Harmony and Conflict
in the Living World

Harmony and Conflict in the Living World

By Alexander F. Skutch

Illustrated by Dana Gardner

UNIVERSITY OF OKLAHOMA PRESS : NORMAN

Also by Alexander F. Skutch and illustrated by Dana Gardner

A Bird Watcher's Adventures in Tropical America (Austin, 1977)
A Naturalist on a Tropical Farm (Berkeley, 1980)
New Studies of Tropical American Birds (Cambridge, Mass., 1981)
Birds of Tropical America (Austin, 1983)
Nature through Tropical Windows (Berkeley, 1983)
Life of the Woodpecker (Ithaca, 1985)
Helpers at Birds' Nests: A Worldwide Survey of Cooperative Breeding and Related Behavior (Iowa City, 1987)
A Naturalist Amid Tropical Splendor (Iowa City, 1987)
Life of the Tanager (Ithaca, 1989)
(with F. Gary Stiles) *A Guide to the Birds of Costa Rica* (Ithaca, 1991)
Life of the Pigeon (Ithaca, 1991)
Origins of Nature's Beauty (Austin, 1992)
The Minds of Birds (College Station, 1996)
Orioles, Blackbirds and Their Kin (Tucson, 1996)
Antbirds and Ovenbirds: Their Lives and Homes (Austin, 1996)
Life of the Flycatcher (Norman, 1997)
Trogons, Laughing Falcons, and Other Neotropical Birds (College Station, 1999)

Library of Congress Cataloging-in-Publication Data

Skutch, Alexander Frank, 1904–
    Harmony and conflict in the living world / by Alexander F. Skutch; illustrated by Dana Gardner.
        p. cm.
    Includes bibliographical refrerences (p.).
    ISBN 0-8061-3231-0 (alk. paper)
    1. Life (Biology)—Philosophy.   I. Title.

QH501 .S54 2000
570'.1—dc21

99-055168

1   2   3   4   5   6   7   8   9   10

Contents

Illustrations

Preface

If I were asked to characterize the living world in one word, the word would be *paradoxical*. A paradox is a conclusion that, although possibly true, appears not to follow logically from its premises, or a situation incompatible with its antecedents. Paradoxes are inconsistencies, contrarieties in the development of a doctrine or a system. The living world, incongruously replete with beauty and ugliness, delight and terror, love and hatred, cooperation and exploitation, life and death, is a fabric of paradoxes.

The most glaring of nature's incongruities is the internecine strife between organisms that, from the least to the greatest, have so much in common. The more intensively they are studied, the more similarities are disclosed, in genetic control and physiological processes, between creatures that vary immensely in form, habitat, and activities. The life and health of each are preserved by a high degree of internal harmony among diverse organs and functions, yet their external relations are frequently far from harmonious.

To understand this paradoxical situation, we must look deeply into the nature of the universe, which, as I explained in *Life Ascending* (1985), is pervaded by an unremitting tendency to arrange its materials in patterns of increasing amplitude, complexity, and coherence—the process of harmonization that brings order out of chaos. On a vast scale it has condensed great quantities of matter, originally present as intergalactic clouds of gases and dust, into stars, planets, and their satellites. It has set the planets in orbits around the stars, the satellites in courses around the planets, in dynamic systems so balanced and stable that, as in our solar system, they endure for long ages.

On a small scale, the same process is evident in the union of atoms in molecules of innumerable kinds, and the alignment of atoms or molecules in enduring crystals that are often of scintillating splendor. In the living world, the tendency of matter to form patterns of increasing amplitude, complexity, and coherence is most clearly revealed in the growth of organisms, even the simpler of which are of greater complexity, and more closely integrated, than anything of comparable size we can find in inorganic nature. The same process is apparent in the moral endeavor to create harmoniously integrated societies, in the efforts of thinkers to form coherent systems of thought, and of artists to create beauty. We owe to harmonization all the values that enhance existence and make life worth living. It appears to be a universal striving to enrich the cosmos by actualizing potentialities, thereby transforming bare Being to full Being, replete with high values.

It is not difficult to understand how strife and suffering arise in a world pervaded by a process that is primarily creative and beneficent. Unguided creativity is unrestrained by moderation. It initiates so many organisms that they compete stubbornly for the space and materials that they need to complete and preserve themselves, with all the lamentable consequences that we have noticed. Not more creativity but more restraint is the world's great need, and this is nowhere more evident than in the human sphere.

In addition to this major paradox, the living world presents many minor ones, a few of which are examined in this book. Among them is the dual nature of animals, products of harmonious development, depending for their survival upon close adjustment to their environments, often dwelling in amity with other creatures, yet capable of such fierce rivalry and lethal violence—contrasts nowhere more glaring than in humankind. Is it not paradoxical that plants, sharply distinguished from animals by their ability to synthesize their own food from inorganic matter as no animal can do, should occasionally turn the tables and devour animals as, on an infinitely larger scale, animals devour plants as well as other animals?

Not the least of the incongruities that the living world presents are revealed by a survey of the growth of intelligence. We might expect reason—the ability to think, to compare, to foresee—to advance steadily from humblest rudiments to full maturity, as a seedling grows into a tree, as daylight brightens from dawn's first glimmer to noontide brilliance, thereby becoming a luminous guide to peaceful living. On the contrary, as chapter 9 tells, our fumbling efforts to use our inchoate rationality have yielded mountains of error and been a major source of absurd practices and widespread suffering.

It is not surprising that serious attempts to understand a confusing living world have led to fantastic interpretations widely accepted by biological orthodoxy. Prominent among those that claim our attention is the doctrine of the "selfish gene," with its corollary that individual animals and plants never act "for the good of the species." Presumably, survival is good, species continue to survive, and what keeps them extant if not the activities of the individuals that compose them? When we reflect that anatomical similarities among diverse animals, such as primates, ungulates, bats, and birds, provide strong evidence for evolution, fervently supported by orthodox biologists, it is puzzling to find them so vehemently rejecting suggestions of psychic resemblances between humans and other creatures, which they condemn as anthropomorphism.

Another scientific heresy is teleology, the ascription of ends or purpose to any part of nature except our very purposeful selves; as though, after a prolonged purposeless preparation for humanity and its manifold material and spiritual needs, purpose suddenly sprang up in the world without antecedents. Equally difficult to understand is the widespread insistence that natural selection acts exclusively upon individuals, never upon populations or groups, apart from which no sexually reproducing organism can propagate its kind.

Chapter 5 compares the consequences of unilateral exploitation with those of cooperation among organisms, noticing the many benefits that we owe to the latter, whereas exploitation has been a major source of life's ills. Finally, we arrive at the paradox that humans, each separated from the surrounding world by a skin that protects his or her finely adjusted vital processes from disastrous intrusions and lethal losses, reach out beyond this insulating integument with love, sympathy, and thirst for understanding that know no bounds.

We look at conservation, which is the effort to halt, or at least to retard, the rapid deterioration of the paradoxical living world, rife with antagonisms and conflicts. This growing enterprise is supported, vocally and often materially, by people with contrasting temperaments and opposing interests. This lack of unanimity is not surprising in a movement that enlists such a diversity of people committed to the preservation of such a perplexing world; conservation is not devoid of its own internal conflicts. Hunters support conservation to ensure a continuing supply of targets for their guns, while friends of animals deplore their needless destruction. Many try to protect, and even increase, the raptors that prey heavily upon the birds, especially Neotropical migrants, whose decline others deplore. Some assign priority to the preservation of habitats, whereas others are more concerned about the fate of species on the verge of extinction. To avoid contrary efforts and waste of inadequate funds, conservationists need to clarify their objectives and agree upon priorities. In chapter 8, I suggest a criterion for conservation that is objective in the sense of being independent of individuals' preference of this or that category of organisms. Widespread adoption of this criterion should greatly promote the ends of conservation.

I wrote this book because I was convinced that examination of some of nature's paradoxes could deepen our understanding of life. Each chapter is an independent essay, understandable without reference to the others; together, they develop a view of the living world that is not despondent but cautiously optimistic. For ready reference, the scientific names of organisms capitalized in the text are given in the index.

Harmony and Conflict
in the Living World

1

A Realm of Paradoxes

What is the most fundamental difference between a living organism—yourself, for example—and a lifeless object, such as a stone? You are self-moved, and the rock is not. You feel and think, as stones evidently cannot do. You are structurally much more complex than any mineral, and your parts are more closely integrated. You are capable of doing a hundred things that stones cannot do. We might continue for pages to enumerate all the ways in which people, and other living things, differ from lifeless things, without hitting upon the most basic difference because it is perhaps the least obvious. I hope that you will not be offended if I suggest that the most fundamental difference between you and a stone is that you are covered by skin and the rock is not. All that the living world has achieved, all its glories and likewise its tragedies, may be traced to the unexciting and sometimes overlooked fact that organisms of all kinds are separated from their ambience by a semipermeable integument, a thin pellicle or a thick skin, such as inorganic objects commonly lack.

INSULATION AND ITS CONSEQUENCES

The basic unit of life is the cell, with the protoplast that it encloses. This consists of the watery, somewhat viscous cytoplasm and the organelles within it, including a nucleus, mitochondria, and various other plastids. Even one-celled organisms, scarcely visible or invisible to our unaided eyes—the amoeba and the paramoecium—are vastly complex. To carry on their diverse functions, they must control their contents, retaining within themselves what they need, resisting the intrusion of superfluous or harmful substances from the surrounding water. They cannot completely insulate themselves from their milieu, for they depend upon it for indispensable materials, and they must return to it waste products of metabolism that would be injurious if permitted to accumulate. To control its exchanges with its surroundings, each minute organism encloses itself in a selectively permeable pellicle or membrane, which freely permits the inward or outward diffusion of certain substances but refuses passage to others. The creature's life depends upon the maintenance of this exceedingly thin and fragile barrier. To impair it is to kill the organism.

Plants and animals increase in complexity by adding cell to cell. Although they cooperate closely, the cells of a multicellular organism preserve a certain independence by retaining the semipermeable ectoplasm that regulates their exchanges with adjoining cells. This is most readily demonstrated in vegetable tissues with cells enclosed in more or less rigid walls of cellulose. Tender growing stems and leaves maintain their shapes while their cells are turgid with water; if they lose too much liquid they wilt and droop, like a balloon from which the air escapes. If one places a thin section of plant tissue in a concentrated solution, as of cane sugar, and watches through a microscope, each protoplast can be seen shrinking away from its enclosing wall of cellulose. The cell's semipermeable ectoplasm permits water to flow outward but retards or prohibits the inward diffusion of the solute. The cytoplast continues to lose water and contract until its osmotic pressure equals that of the solution in which it is immersed.

In addition to the defenses of their individual cells, multicellular organisms develop more obvious and resistant means of regulating their exchanges with their media. Trunks, branches, and roots of woody plants cover themselves with bark, which at least on younger branches is penetrated by lenticels more permeable to air. Leaves and herbaceous stems are covered with waxy cuticles, which are thicker and less permeable to water the more arid the environment. Penetrating the cuticle and epidermis of leaves and green stems are multitudes of minute pores, the stomata, which by opening and closing regulate the inward and outward passage of gases needed for respiration and photosynthesis, and the outward diffusion of water vapor in transpiration.

The integuments of animals are wonderfully diverse. Many aquatic and not a few terrestrial creatures enclose themselves in hard shells or carapaces, which may have evolved primarily for protection from predators but at the same time help to insulate animals from the ambience. Insects are covered by their chitinous exoskeletons, penetrated by the tracheal openings through which they breathe. Among vertebrates, the primary integument is a flexible skin, resistant to most substances that are likely to moisten it in an animal's natural environment, constantly renewed as it wears away, and in many animals equipped with sweat glands that help to regulate body temperature, or with chromatophores that by changing its color assimilate to the background and make the wearer less conspicuous to enemies. The scales of fish and reptiles, the hair of mammals, and the feathers of birds give additional protection.

Although every organism from algae and protozoa to trees and the largest vertebrates can regulate the entrance and exit of materials to and from its living cells, only fur and feathers, or subcutaneous fat in certain animals of cold climates, provide effective thermal insulation. Only animals covered with hair or feathers that enclose many minute air spaces can afford the luxury of constant body temperature; for others, the attempt to achieve homeothermy would cost too much energy. By growing a thicker coat of feathers or fur as the climate becomes colder, or depositing more fat beneath their skins, birds and mammals can remain warm and active in air so frigid that all other creatures become dormant or die. They have attained the maximum independence from climatic extremes that animals can achieve without shelters that can be heated or cooled.

Insulation is not only physical but also psychic. We do not doubt that other people feel, and sometimes think, much as we ourselves do; and the more intimately we study the lives of other animals, the more certain we become that they, too, are stirred by emotions and are not devoid of thought. But, with certain possible and debatable exceptions, we never have direct, unassailable evidence that other creatures of any kind feel or think; we infer their feelings and thoughts from the way they act, the sounds they emit, their facial expressions. Our psychic insulation is tighter than our physical insulation; the membranes that separate us from our physical environment are but semipermeable, permitting many substances to pass in and out; whatever it may be that shields our minds from direct awareness of the psychic states of other creatures is nearly, if not wholly, impermeable. This insulation makes it possible for one animal to harm another without feeling the consequences.

Although we seldom attribute sociality to lifeless things, they are in fact much more social than living organisms. They seldom enclose themselves in integuments that, like walls, effectively separate them from surrounding materials but freely intermingle when they meet. Rocks and crystals expose their unmodified substance, their naked bodies, to the disintegrative action of air, water, and soil. Gasses of different kinds intermingle, or are absorbed by liquids, with usually no barrier to control the process. Drops of a liquid coalesce when they flow together, one losing its identity in the other. Even solids such as metals slowly diffuse through each other when tightly pressed together. Everywhere in inorganic nature we find readiness to meet and to mingle; no substance appears to be consistently averse to losing its distinctness by union with some other substance. Rarely do we find such aloofness, such stubborn clinging to a separate and insulated existence, as in living things. It is significant that when we wish to waterproof a fabric, or to cover metal or wood with a thin, impermeable pellicle that will shield it from rust or decay, we commonly choose for the protective coating some substance elaborated by living organisms. Waxes, resins, rubber, in their many varieties, are not fortuitous secretions of plants; they are elaborated for the protection of vegetable bodies.

With the exceptions of parasites and their hosts, only exceptionally do separate organisms unite as intimately as lifeless substances so frequently do, and these are nearly always members of the same species. Relatively simple animalcules, like corals and sponges, join in large numbers to form compound organisms. Roots of different trees of the same species, especially conifers, may fuse together when they meet in the soil, and the horticulturist's art may graft one variety of a tree or shrub upon the stock of another. The higher animals so stubbornly resist the intrusion into their own flesh of alien flesh, even of their own species, that only by the surgeon's utmost art can they be induced to accept a foreign organ to replace a diseased one of their own.

Even in their manner of destruction, living beings demonstrate their essential difference from the nonliving. Barring violent impacts and such crushing forces as might reduce rocks and crystals to rubble or powder and living flesh to formless pulp, organic and inorganic bodies are destroyed in radically different ways. Rocks weather on their exposed surfaces and slowly dwindle; crystals dissolve from the surface inward; drops of a liquid evaporate from the outside. But living things are so well enclosed in protective membranes or integuments that their destruction, when not caused by violence or high temperatures, usually results from changes in the interior rather than at the surface. The deadly poison or fatal parasite must insinuate its way into the body, either through one of the natural openings normally under the control of the organism or through a break in its integument, before it can begin its work of destruction. Or, if it escape death in other forms, the organism runs down and becomes quiescent from senescence, a process wholly internal.

The other distinctive qualities of living organisms are ancillary to their ceaseless effort to preserve separate identity. Most significant of these are their capacity to assimilate and incorporate intimately into themselves materials different from their own substance, and to grow from within rather than at the surface—by intussusception rather than by apposition, as botanists say. Whereas crystals and other inorganic bodies that do not enclose themselves in insulating membranes may continue to grow by means of superficial deposits, this method of enlargement is not available to an insulated organic body.

Living things tend to avoid contact with substances and processes that would harm them: a protozoan swims away from the diffusing chemical that would kill it; a man snatches his hand away from a hot stove. Inorganic bodies show no comparable tendency to avoid other bodies that would injure them. But the living organism does not always passively await actual contact with the deleterious substance; it displays a sensitivity to influences playing upon it, from sources near or remote, such as is rarely found in inorganic matter, and frequently it succeeds in escaping from dangerous situations. And when contact with the injurious foreign object is inevitable, it exhibits an ability to adapt itself, to escape destruction by changing shape and endless stratagems, for which one looks in vain in lifeless bodies.

But in spite of all its defenses and its wiliness in confronting unfavorable situations, the more highly differentiated organism must sooner or later succumb, if not by external agency, then by internal decay. Yet even mortality cannot defeat it. If it cannot maintain its separateness in its own body, it will transmit this capacity for preserving separateness to others like itself—not only to one, but to several or many, to ensure the perpetuation of its kind against all contingencies. As though foreseeing its own eventual disintegration, it does this while still at the flood tide of vitality, while senescence and death seem remote. The capacity to reproduce itself in all its complexity, from a minute and seemingly simple particle of itself, is one of the most marvelous of all the properties of the living organism, and one that strongly distinguishes organic from inorganic bodies. Although the latter sometimes display superficial resemblances to the life processes, analysis shows that these seeming likenesses in inorganic substances are not close.

TOUGHNESS AND AGGRESSIVENESS OF LIFE

A great paradox of living substance is its combination of tenacity with extreme frailty. It is so easy to destroy by heat, by intense illumination, by chemicals of a thousand kinds, by mechanical violence;

yet with incredible Protean cunning living things outwit destroyers and blossom forth again with renewed vigor and fertility. A rock in your field is troublesome; you carry it away and see it no more. But pull up a weed, remove it, burn it, grind it into fragments, utterly obliterate it—and the chances are that within a few months, seeds or fragments of it that escaped your notice will have produced a hundred weeds where you found one. To emphasize the evanescence of human life, moralists sometimes ask where are the hands that erected the Pyramids or built the Parthenon. Where are they, indeed? Those hands are multiplied a thousandfold; they are in Europe and America and Africa and Australia and on the farthest islands of the oceans; while the stones that they set in place daily dwindle under the action of wind, rain, and frost.

A fundamental property of life is its stubbornness, its opposition to the forces that would carry it away, reduce it, or annihilate it. The swiftly flowing river bears downward, for yards or miles, a stick, a stone, or any other lifeless thing that may fall into it; but all its free-swimming living inhabitants, from great fish to frail beetles and striders and other organisms so small that they escape the careless eye, set their heads resolutely against the current and resist its force. The fish in the mountain torrent is symbolic of all life, in the water, on the ground, or in the air: it resists the forces that would carry it along. Life seems to be pitted against the external world; struggle is its essence. And although against cataclysmic forces it is pathetically helpless, tossed like a feather by the tempest, burnt to cinders by a puff of volcanic vapor, for all its frailty it is the toughest thing under the Sun.

To add to the paradox, this thing at once so delicate and so resistant, so ephemeral and so enduring, tends ever to clothe itself in forms that present a greater challenge to all that is inimical in its environment, as though exulting in opposition to elemental forces and delighting to devise new ways of thwarting them. To the seaweed floating in still water, the maintenance of life is relatively simple. Constantly bathed in a liquid containing all that it needs for respiration and growth, it is hardly affected by the pull of gravitation; neither scorching sunshine nor drying wind is a

threat to it; it has no occasion to send forth roots to gather essential elements thinly diffused through the soil, then transport them
to distant organs.

Why did not vegetation remain forever content with the security of the aquatic environment in which it arose? What stubborn
perversity of the living substance goaded it into invading the land,
into assuming forms the continued existence of which is a miracle
of audacity? In every respect in which life is simple and safe for the
seaweed, it is complex and perilous for the tree. Whereas the alga
vegetates in a caressing bath of nutrient fluid, the tree rears its lofty
head as though to defy the gales and the lightning, the drying winds
and the desiccating sunlight, the unremitting gravitational pull of
Earth. It is endlessly extracting water and solutes from the soil and,
by a process that has been difficult to understand, raising them fifty
or a hundred yards into the air. It ceaselessly resists the elemental
forces that would dry up its sap, starve its living foliage, and flatten
it on the ground. And yet, as though to testify to the toughness and
enterprise of life, trees, not algae, are (or until recently were) the
dominant vegetation on this planet.

In the animal kingdom, the course of evolution has paralleled
that of plants. Life is simple for the amoeba and other blobs of
protoplasm that live always immersed in the water that forms the
greater part of their substance; but as we all know, life is complicated for humans in our multiform, constantly changing environment. The more we contemplate the transformation, the more
incredible it appears that organisms forsook the ease and security
(except from other organisms) of their primitive aquatic ambience
to live unquietly amid all the stresses and perils of the less stable
aerial environment. Had they been forced by some external power
to assume forms whose preservation demands ever-increasing effort,
their metamorphosis would have been surprising enough. We mar-
vel the more when we remember that the impulse that drove them
from change to change has always come from within them.

It is not that the universe, or that immediately effective part of
it that we call the environment, is actively hostile to life, as Bertrand
Russell (1917) believed. Save for an occasional hurricane, volcanic
eruption, or flood, the environment is passive enough. In many

regions, it is so favorable for vital processes that it almost seems to invite the presence of living things. Its fitness to support them has many aspects. Water is, of all known liquids, that which best serves as a medium for intricate processes that can go forward only within a narrow range of temperatures; and it is the only liquid abundantly present on the surface of our planet. Among the properties that make it a fit medium for life are its high specific heat, which retards changes in temperature; its abrupt change from contraction to expansion as, in cooling, it approaches the freezing point, which causes it to congeal from the surface downward rather than from the bottom upward and increases the thermal stability at low temperatures of deep lakes and seas, making their complete congelation improbable. Add to this its chemical stability combined with its versatility as a solvent, and its capacity to form, with carbon, compounds rich in latent energy. Likewise oxygen, hydrogen, nitrogen, the sunlight, and the soil all have properties that make them peculiarly favorable for vital processes. The environment is friendly enough to life.

Life, on the other hand, often seems to challenge or defy the environment, like an aggressor invading a hostile land. Had it been content to remain in the warm seas where it began, in the humid tropical lands where today it flourishes most lushly, it might have existed in vast profusion yet remained in friendly inorganic surroundings. But not satisfied with these immense yet almost uniformly congenial domains, restless life, impelled by its own great capacity for multiplication, invaded the arid deserts, advanced far toward Earth's frigid poles, climbed ever higher up rocky mountain slopes, battling against thin air and intense insolation and cruelly sudden changes in temperature. On every front, life armed itself to battle with the environment, which is not intentionally cold or arid or changeable—seized it by the throat, so to speak, and by sheer force compelled it to yield what imperious life needed and demanded. When conflict arises between life and its milieu, life is usually the aggressor; the passive environment is what it must be.

In these uncongenial regions where intrusive life exists precariously, a slight intensification of the prevailing conditions, such as more prolonged drought in an arid land or exceptionally intense cold in a frigid zone, causes great destruction of living things. We are then apt to remark upon the harshness or cruelty of nature. But can one who perversely sits too close to the fire claim to be unfairly treated if scorched now and then?

It was once the habit to look upon all those features of Earth that make it a favorable home for living things as special provisions for this end. This interpretation provided a strong argument for natural theology, and writers of this school became eloquent as they contemplated the manifold arrangements that make this planet a congenial abode for humankind. Since the publication of *The Origin of Species* in 1859, an exactly contrary view has become current. It is now held that we must not regard any features of the physical world as adaptations to support life; but that life, the late-comer, has simply had to conform to the conditions it found here, which it accomplished by a long course of trial and error.

This interpretation is as wide of the mark as the earlier one. It would be true only if life owed its origin to a process wholly different from that which formed the lifeless world, or if it had somehow intruded into this world from beyond. But since it is a product of the same process—harmonization—that earlier prepared the stage for it, this modern view is obviously too extreme. Actually, the living world is related to the physical world as one phase of a continuous process to an earlier phase. Life is adapted to its inorganic setting because it emerged from that setting; the setting is adapted to life because it was formed by a preceding phase of the movement that gave rise to life. The adaptation is neither all on the side of the environment nor all on the side of life, but the conformity is that of the parts to the whole.

Life's stubborn intrusion into environments poorly fitted to support it reveals the intensity of harmonization's striving to build up patterns of higher integration, even in the face of the utmost obstacles. By far the greater part of the stuff of the universe is prevented by physical conditions from attaining the level of organization found in living things. Only an infinitesimal proportion of the total quantity of matter can at one time participate in such complex formations. Yet the moment it encounters favorable circumstances, the stuff of the universe rushes with unrestrained exuberance to arrange itself in elaborate patterns, exhibiting closer integration and greater beauty than we often detect in the lifeless world. A major portion of life's ills springs from just this almost explosive rush by the cosmic stuff to participate in a higher synthesis; if this urge did not result in such excessive numbers of organisms, life would certainly be more pleasant for those endowed with it.

CONFLICTS BETWEEN ORGANISMS

Just as they are often militant against the environment, living things are belligerent toward one another. One organism invades another, forcing it to yield the requisites of its own existence, to become a living environment for it. Nothing is sacred; no organ, tissue, or fluid, no matter how exquisitely delicate and admirably adapted to an intricate function, no matter how indispensable to the life of the host, is spared the pitiless invasion. Eyes and ears, heart and lungs, the very lifeblood itself—all are at times forced to become the medium of aggressive foreign organisms. Myriads of creatures live parasitically at the expense of others, from viruses too minute to be detected by common microscopes to ticks and leeches that batten shamelessly in view of all the world.

A growing organism tends to perfect a form intimately related to its mode of life and the constants of its natural environment. Except where strong winds prevail, trees commonly form upright trunks surrounded by boughs arranged with radial symmetry. Encrusting lichens spread in expanding circles over the faces of rocks. The giant kelp assumes an elongate, flattened form that permits it to yield gracefully to the ceaseless surge and tug of the surf where it thrives. Not only the organism as a whole but each organ strives to express its innate form or pattern; each leaf, according to its position on the herb or tree, would if left to itself become an undistorted example of its hereditary type. Likewise, each animal tends to become a shapely representative of its kind, perfect of limb and organ, its garment of scales or fur or feathers comely and complete in every detail. Nevertheless, countless creatures fail to attain the full perfection of which they are capable.

When we investigate the causes of the failure of organisms to be whole and perfect examples of their kind, we usually find that other living things, rather than the inorganic setting, are to blame. As a rule, the environment cooperates with the organism, helping it to perfect the form that was evolved in relation to this same environment. But it is quite the contrary with living things; they rarely modify their innate tendencies to grow to full perfection so that neighboring organisms may do likewise. They crowd and push against each other until shapeliness is impossible; they twine around and constrict each other; they strive to live in such egregious numbers that none of the multitude can procure all that it needs for full development; they invade each other's vital tissues; they consume each other piecemeal or devour each other whole. So intense is the struggle that, in tropical forests, a botanist may often search through the whole crown of some great fallen tree without finding a single twig with perfect foliage for his collection—insects have gnawed into all of them even before they stopped growing. It is only exceptionally that the environment prevents organisms from attaining their ideal form; it is far more often the strife between the living things themselves.

Yet, except among morally underdeveloped people, we rarely find a suggestion that one living thing injures another just for the sake of hurting or destroying it. Each is striving to maintain and complete itself, to realize that particular perfection inherent in its own organization, but its circumstances are often such that it cannot procure all the materials or the space it needs for this purpose without opposing or injuring other living things. Life is always primarily constructive; destruction is all too often incidental to its activity but hardly its primary goal. Thus, each living thing owes its being to an organizing movement and its continued existence to the maintenance of a harmoniously integrated pattern, yet it must ever be prepared to contend with or to resist other more or less similar entities. These opposing tendencies account for those contradictions in the character of animals that claim our attention in chapter 3.

REAL STRIFE CONFINED TO THE LIVING WORLD

By the efforts of living things to occupy environments unfavorable to vital processes, and even more by the clash of organism with organism in a crowded world, harmonization, itself a definite, straightforward movement, becomes entangled in organic evolution, a labyrinth of complexities and contradictions that confuse the student of nature. We shall not succeed in understanding evolution unless we distinguish clearly between its driving force and true constructive principle, harmonization, and the dreadful embroilment into which the living world is plunged by the manifold interactions of evolution's products. Without this distinction, the living world appears to be a fantastic welter of competing forms, a maze of frenzied stirrings leading nowhere; only in this light can we hope to discover a path through the labyrinth (Skutch 1985).

Life has needed to be aggressive because it has had to make its own way, creating itself under the constant impulsion of harmonization working within it. Evolution is self-creation. The origin of species by gradual evolution implies their formation by their own efforts. External agents have dictated the forms that organisms must assume in order to survive, but they have not made these organisms. Beyond the primitive home of life in tepid seas and humid adjoining lands, external agents would have annihilated living things but for their stubborn drive to exist. The environment has everywhere stipulated the conditions that organisms must accept if they would continue to live, but it has not itself altered them into conformity with these conditions. On the contrary, living things have molded themselves to their medium like some soft, plastic creature or tissue, an octopus or a growing root, forcing itself into a crevice in the rock, pressing itself home until it fits snugly into every cranny and around every projection. It is not the rock, but the octopus or the root, that has supplied the energy for this close adaptation.

The genesis of species by gradual changes promoted by interactions between themselves, surrounding organisms, and the physical environment provides a key to the understanding of evil. As long as people believed that each kind of living thing had been created in its finished form by an Agent at once omnipotent and beneficent, strife and evil remained inexplicable, or could be explained only by means of unconvincing myths. For a Creator of unlimited power and perfect benevolence might have established each species in all its perfection, adjusting the relations of each one to every other, and of every one to its environment, so harmoniously that strife and discord would never arise. Actually, however, they have been self-created, formed by this very attrition and interplay that special creation might have obviated.

Apart from life, the disharmony we behold in the universe is more seeming then real. Matter flows ceaselessly from form to form; body collides with body; the smaller mass fuses with the greater and loses separate identity. Solar systems no less than molecules are constantly changing, dying, being born anew. No composite thing is eternal, nothing immutable, nothing fixed for all time. Strife has been called cosmic; but are the collisions and the often violent transformations that we witness in lifeless matter actually strife? Strife is essentially a conflict of wills, an attempt to alter or destroy that which stubbornly strives to preserve its present form. But in inorganic matter we detect no strong will to exist as a separate entity. Lifeless bodies rarely sheathe themselves in an insulating integument as in a coat of armor; it appears immaterial to the crystal, the rock, the mountain, the planet, or the solar system whether it continue in its present form or be transmuted to something else. These compound bodies evidently lack the will to perpetuate themselves. Far from resisting the closest union with others, the micropsychic atoms of which they are composed readily seek such union to satisfy their social nature.

"Cosmic strife" would be more aptly characterized as a cosmic dance. The dancers are marshaled in companies of the most diverse sizes—of atoms, molecules, crystals, drops, oceans, continents, planets, solar systems, and galaxies. Each company is ceaselessly shifting its place, meeting others and uniting with them; or else great armies separate into smaller bands. And within each company the platoons, squads, and individuals are in constant happy agitation, following the immutable rules of the dance. In all the vast concourse, everyone appears to be in a tranquil mood; there are, as far as we can discern, no hatred, no anger, no jealousy, no vain strivings, no sighs, no regrets—no tragedy evident to our human eyes and minds. Strife springs from individuality, from the effort to preserve separate identity by beings that try to insulate themselves from the rest of the universe and that are not minutely guided by a single comprehensive Intelligence.

Contemplating the countless ills that arise directly from organisms' need to insulate themselves from their surroundings, one sometimes suspects that life represents a miscarriage of harmonization, which in producing living things somehow went astray. Yet the very intensity of the movement to create them and lift them to higher levels of organization suggests that they are indispensable for the fulfillment of the world process. It seems that only in a community of individuals can harmony, in its highest sense, prevail. If harmony were simply unruffled uniformity, such as is found in a body of pure, still water or among the pages of a closed book, the whole creative process is a mistake; for the longer it continues, the farther it carries the world from this condition. Harmony is unity in diversity, concord between differing entities. Whether in a work of art or a society, the more varied the entities that compose it, the richer and more precious their harmonious integration becomes. For the higher modes of harmony, individuality appears to be indispensable; and the physiological foundation of individuality is the insulation of organisms. Spiritual community is superimposed on this biological separation; it owes its sweetness and poignancy to its persistent striving to overcome the very aloofness that is its foundation. Moreover, as far as we can tell, only individuals can experience happiness and high values, toward which the whole creative process appears to be directed.

COOPERATION AND COMPETITION

Furthermore, we must be careful lest by overemphasizing the strife of the living world we lose sight of its complementary aspect. Those who see in nature only battle and carnage are as shortsighted as

those who find there only beauty and peace. Each of these interpretations results from a need to discover in nature support for one's
own dominant mood; so that to the violent and bloodthirsty, nature
is red in tooth and claw, while to the loving heart she is the tender
universal mother. This capacity to give to each that which he or she
seeks is proof of nature's vast diversity.

The outstanding feature of the relations between organisms,
whether of the same or of diverse kinds, is neither their friendliness nor their hostility so much as their baffling complexity. On
one hand, organisms must cooperate closely to create and stabilize
the environment on which the prosperity of each of them depends.
On the other hand, they are forced to compete for materials, space,
and energy, which are rarely abundant enough to fill the needs of
all the individuals produced by life's prodigious powers of multiplication. Cooperation and competition, harmony and strife are
equally prominent in life's paradoxical involvement. Those who
blindly stress one of these contrasting aspects while forgetting the
other have not understood life. Cooperation and competition are
so intimately linked that it is hardly possible to separate them.
Cooperators readily become competitors, and competitors may
become cooperators before they are aware of it, both in natural
communities and the commercial human world. Stranger still, it
often happens that the same creatures are simultaneously cooperators and competitors; as, by their very competition, the rule-
abiding players of two opposing teams provide the cooperation
that makes a good game.

The more complex organisms, animal and even vegetable, can
hardly survive in a lifeless milieu. The cooperation of many of
them is needed to create a favorable environment. Yet these same
organisms compete with, and often destroy, one another. A mature
forest, for example, in large measure creates its own environment.
Closely spaced trees are necessary to prepare and preserve the
peculiar qualities of soil, humidity, and light requisite for the germi-
nation and prosperous growth of these same trees. Nevertheless,
they compete keenly for space, mineral nutrients, and sunlight.
Many lose in this struggle and die. Swarming insects devour the
foliage of the trees, yet some of these trees need some of the insects

to pollinate their flowers. The saprophytic fungi that break down dead wood and foliage, returning mineral nutrients to the soil and enriching the mold necessary for the continued growth of the vegetation, readily mutate into parasitic strains that attack living plants. The birds roaming through the forest in mixed flocks help one another to detect and escape enemies and to find food but compete for the food thus encountered. If food becomes scarce, as in temperate-zone forests in winter, competition grows keen and some individuals may starve because their more competent companions capture the larger share. So delicate and so paradoxical is the balance between cooperation and competition! Nowhere is this paradox more striking than in the world of humans, who so need one another's support yet are so often mutually hostile.

There was a time when an intelligent observer of events on this planet might have suspected that the process of creation at multiple centers had reached an impasse, a point where cooperation and harmony could not be increased without at the same time intensifying competition and discord; and competition could not be diminished without at the same time reducing the number and quality of existing organisms. For the more highly organized the creature, the more it needs the cooperation and support of a complex environment, yet the more it preys on or competes with the very organisms that make its own life possible. Although nearly every living creature is in some respects a cooperator and in some respects a competitor with its neighbors, the latter is perhaps more evident in its behavior. Its instincts and appetites are directed primarily toward its own welfare, prompting it to seek what it needs without much consideration for its neighbors. Only toward its mate and dependent young, and more rarely toward other members of its flock or herd, is it explicitly altruistic. Yet by the secular interactions of species in living communities, the habits of each become compatible with the survival of associated species, in so far as this is necessary to preserve the biotic association in a thriving state. Species that cause the deterioration of their environment dig the ground from beneath their feet and prepare their own doom.

To break the impasse between cooperation and competition and turn the balance in favor of harmony, only one hope is at present discernible on this planet. Very recently, as cosmic and even terrestrial time are measured, beings gifted with free intelligence and morality arose upon it. At first, these faculties were dedicated exclusively to the welfare of the individual animals endowed with them and their close kin, but gradually they acquired a broader vision. When leavened with sympathy, intelligence can understand the way of life of other creatures, their needs and tendencies. Taking the external view, intelligent beings can often predict at what points others will come into conflict with themselves, and sometimes they can also foresee how such conflicts might be avoided, or at least mitigated. They can guide the formation of patterns from two or more centers simultaneously toward eventual harmonious union, in a manner impossible to an immanent creative process that can work only from within.

Morality at its best is willingness to modify one's own life and reduce one's material needs so that other beings may fulfill themselves. As long as life can be sustained only by exploiting an environment that can never satisfy all the demands made upon it by teeming creatures, strife and conflict will never be wholly eliminated. But moral effort, inspired by love and directed by intelligence, can do much to diminish disorder and promote harmony. A person becomes the more eager to dedicate his strength to this endeavor when he reflects that the contrast between himself and the beings that surround him is not nearly as sharp as it appears to minds that spontaneously exaggerate distinctions in the interest of effective action. Humans so endowed, who devote themselves to this cause, become voluntary workers in the cause of harmony, impelled to undertake this high endeavor by their sensitivity to the creative energy within them, their loyalty to the process that made them. At all levels of the world process we detect a tendency to overcome conflicts by the union of colliding patterns in a higher synthesis, but it is by means of moral agents of this high quality that harmonization most readily overcomes strife between physiologically and psychically insulated organisms not directly sensible to the pain or distress that one too often inflicts upon another.

2

The Individual and Its Species

Before we explore the relation of the individual to its species, we must clarify the nature of a species. The textbook that I studied early in this century in my first college course in general biology asserted that "a species is merely a concept of the human mind—the only reality in nature is the individual, and an understanding of the differences between individuals gives us a key to the differences between species." This nonminalist position conforms to the definition of a species as a group of individuals "which differ less among themselves in the sum of their characters than they do from the members of any other group of individuals" (Woodruff 1922). One might make a similar statement about human artifacts; the word *chairs*, for example, denotes a group of objects that differ less among themselves than they do from other kinds of household furniture. But chairs are related to each other only ideally; they conform to a concept in our minds; one chair does not create another. If all the chairs in the world were to be destroyed tomorrow, furniture makers would be so busy that, after a few months, there would be no lack of chairs. When a biological species is exterminated, it can never be replaced.

The definition of species in my college textbook is close to the original concept of a species as a class of objects that look alike, as, with due regard to age and sex, the members of a biological species mostly do. Early systematists, including Linnaeus, regarding species as unchanging entities, each corresponding to a Platonic form or an idea in the mind of God, depended largely upon their outward aspect, sometimes supplemented by a study of their anatomy, to delimit them. As is evident from the foregoing quotation, widespread acceptance of Darwin's theory of evolution did not immediately change this. More recently, the old morphological concept of species has been superseded by a more realistic, dynamic view. The biological concept of a species, now widely used in classification, regards it as a group of individuals that freely breed together wherever they intermingle, producing fertile progeny. Spontaneous interbreeding is a more dependable indication of specific limits than is the production of fertile offspring by artificial crossing. The former depends upon the appearance and behavior of animals; the latter, upon the compatibility of their genetic complexes, which is a quite different matter.

Extreme forms of a species may differ so conspicuously in appearance as to be placed in separate species, as in the case of Baltimore and Bullock's orioles, variously considered separate or lumped together as Northern Orioles; or that of Yellow-shafted and Red-shafted flickers, now united as Northern Flickers. On the other hand, forms too similar to be readily distinguished may by classified as different species if they fail to interbreed where they are in contact, as is true of a number of American flycatchers. Since we think so much about genes nowadays, we might define a species as a group of individuals who share a common pool of genes, a selection of which is present, in diverse combinations, in each of them. All members of a species are descended from the same ancestral stock; a species is monophyletic. When we view a species in this biological rather than in the formalistic manner, it becomes clear that it is not merely a concept of the human mind but a self-perpetuating natural entity, no less real than the individuals that compose it. Indeed, if reality has degrees, and the longer something exists the more real it is, species have greater reality than individuals, which are to their species as leaves to a tree.

One may ask why animals and plants belong to species that are typically sharply delimited from other species instead of intergrading so that they might be arranged in series without discontinuities, in which case we might, for example, find every possible gradation between an Ostrich and a hummingbird, or an oak tree and a violet. Probably, if all the organisms that have become extinct through the ages were presently available, we might come close to doing this, but in no single era would this be feasible. In the geographical races of many species, we do indeed find a gradual transition between extreme forms, which do not, however, transcend the limits of a species. Between species, especially those in the same region, gaps of some kind are always present.

The discontinuities in the living world are closely related to biparental reproduction. To reproduce sexually, organisms must find partners whose genetic constitutions, called genomes, are compatible. This is the fundamental reason why plants and animals belong to species. In a world where asexual propagation predominated, instead of being subordinate to sexual reproduction as in our actual world, we might indeed find all transitions between the most extreme types, as on a small scale we do among cultivated plants. And how confusing this would be to everyone interested in nature, how frustrating to all attempts to classify and name! The biological definition of a species as a group of individuals any two adults of which, of opposite sex and normally developed, might together beget fertile progeny, recognizes the intimate connection between biparental reproduction and the segregation of organisms into species. By this definition, cultivated plants that can be propagated only vegetatively, such as certain varieties of bananas and sugarcane and many ornamentals, are clones that do not properly belong in any species, although for convenience they are classified in the species from which they were apparently derived. With these exceptions, individuals and species are mutually dependent; neither can persist without the other.

The publication two decades ago of Richard Dawkins's *The Selfish Gene* (1976) has helped to diffuse the idea, implicit in much contemporary thought about evolution, that the individual does nothing "for the good of its species." We need only to recall the interdependence of individual and species to recognize the logical absurdity of this perverse notion. If to exist is good, and if the existence of any composite entity, such as a species, depends upon its parts, then, simply by existing, individuals contribute to the good of their species. But living organisms commonly do more than contribute passively to the existence of their species, as parts of some lifeless object, a chair or a machine, contribute to its wholeness; by reproducing they perpetuate their species in a perilous world. Reproduction benefits not the reproductive individual but the progeny, few or many, that will continue to compose the species. Unless the parent finds satisfaction in rearing young, as apparently some do, or unless when grown the offspring promotes a parent's comfort or safety, as is rare in the animal kingdom, the individual gains nothing by reproducing. It squanders vital resources, exposes itself to dangers that it might avoid if careful only of its own safety, often exhausts itself, and shortens its life to perpetuate its species, as does the salmon when, after struggling upstream against foaming rapids, she lays her eggs and expires.

Modern evolutionary thought is preoccupied with the competition among organisms of the same species to increase their fitness, measured by the number of their living progeny. Successful individuals often deprive others of mates or opportunities to reproduce, sometimes of their lives. Responsibility for this selfishness is frequently attributed to the organisms' genes. However, if an individual's genes increase its fitness, their multiplication, even if this entails the exclusion of the less efficient genes of competing organisms, benefits the species, which thereby becomes more firmly established in the living world. In competing with others of their kind for the means of reproduction, individuals appear to vie with one another to contribute to their species. The great majority of organisms can serve their species only by producing offspring; but more social animals can otherwise benefit their kind, as by mutual aid, joining in constructive enterprises, teaching, creating, inventing, or clarifying thoughts and ideals—these last, of course, only in humans. Paradoxically, by "selfishly" striving to increase the number of their progeny, individuals may benefit their species more than themselves. However, animals contributing too many offspring to their species may harm it by overburdening the habitat and causing widespread starvation. Even in beneficial activities, moderation is needed.

Apart from mutations that might arise in its reproductive tissues, the genes an organism bears are not peculiarly its own but were inherited from its forebears, which are seen to be more numerous the farther backward in time we trace its ancestry. The more these genes contribute to the quality of the individual and the survival of its race, the more their bearer serves its species by transmitting to posterity this endowment which, in a sense, it holds in trust for future generations.

An animal may serve its species without assisting its contemporaries, or it may aid them without benefit to its species, as is particularly evident in human society, where philanthropy or charity, no less than medical aid, may have highly dysgenic consequences. Beneficence too often helps incompetent individuals with heritable defects not only to survive but to beget children who are likely to receive the undesirable traits of their parents, thereby deteriorating the human stock. We value the impulse to help the unfortunate, while we deplore consequences that might be avoided if those with genetic defects who are made comfortable by public or private assistance could be restrained from reproduction; if they desire children, they might adopt one or two. Animals in a state of nature commonly lack the surplus of energy and resources to succor less fortunate or less well endowed individuals, nor can they afford to weaken their species by diluting its gene pool with inferior genes. Failure to distinguish behavior beneficial to the species from that which aids individuals most in need of support has led certain biologists to exaggerate the selfishness of animals, or of the genes that determine their behavior.

Some animals act in ways that are excessively brutal, as when male lions or langurs destroy the suckling young of a female wrested from another male, so that the mother may the sooner become pregnant with the winner's progeny; or when a victorious human tribe massacres all the males and pregnant females among its captives, retaining the virgins to bear children for their captors, as happened when the Israelites, at the command of their leader, Moses, overcame the Midianites (Numbers 31).

Such harshness has rarely been recorded in the animal world. More widespread is the mitigation of conflict by ritualization, especially among birds, which tend to settle disputes by posturing and calling rather than by fighting. At territorial boundaries, howling monkeys of tropical American forests confront their neighbors with stentorian voices that obviate physical clashes. Or if fighting becomes serious, the losing animal may save itself by assuming a submissive posture that pacifies its opponent, as happens among wolves, turkeys, and gulls. Natural selection should promote all behavior that abbreviates or avoids conflicts that needlessly squander the contestants' energy and expose them to predation while they struggle, heedless of what is happening around them. Few species are so firmly established that they can afford to lose many members in intraspecific strife. Predation and parasitism, far more than competition between individuals of a species, make nature harsh and bloody.

Many animals increase their safety by joining in flocks or herds, composed of one or more species. Although mixed flocks of birds foraging through tropical woodland are conspicuous, many keen eyes and voices ready to sound the alarm make them difficult for a predator to approach undetected. By joining such flocks, a bird apparently feels, and is, safer than if it lurked obscurely amid dense vegetation. In the midst of a compact flock, foraging in trees or on the ground, birds spend more time eating, less looking around or up to avoid being surprised by predators, than do individuals on the outskirts of the crowd, or those foraging alone. In these aggregations, each individual tries primarily to protect itself and increase its intake of food; but by the combined action of all, all are safer and better nourished. Because no individual willingly exposes itself to save its companions, or deliberately helps an adult not its mate to food, these foraging groups are sometimes called "selfish herds." But is it not enough that by acting in concert the whole party benefits? Why should one individual court death to save another adult of its species? Large animals, well armed with horns, hoofs, or fangs—zebras, horned ungulates, baboons—may save companions or dependent young by confronting powerful predators; small, weak creatures could only sacrifice themselves.

Protection from predators is the most widespread mode of mutual aid among animals. The startled cries of a bird that spies a hawk alert others within hearing, of the same or different species. These notes, frequently voiced by birds with or without dependent young, have puzzled evolutionists who believe that animals should consistently behave in ways conducive to individual survival and fitness. Why should a bird that first notices an approaching raptor draw attention to itself by its voice, when it might discreetly hide, leaving less alert companions exposed to attack? Perhaps among the birds warned by its cries are its mate or independent young, in which case its behavior is more readily explicable. But a bird may sound the alarm when no related individual is within hearing, and birds of other species may be saved by this timely warning. To be sure, the individual giving the alarm call may on another occasion profit by that of some other bird; its service may be requited. Except in the context of parents with young, alarm cries have proved difficult for evolutionists to reconcile with their theories, but they obviously benefit the caller's species by promoting the safety of its members— and often those of other species.

The great majority of birds breed in monogamous pairs, of which the male feeds and guards the young, or frequently shares with his mate all the activities of the nest, including building, incubating, and brooding the nestlings. In a minority of species, females are so well able to rear their families without help that the males are released from all domestic chores. By staying aloof, they decrease activity that might reveal nests to hostile eyes. Instead of remaining alone, the emancipated males of a number of species gather in courtship assembles, which attract females whose developing eggs need to be fertilized. Among northern birds, this mating system is followed by certain sandpipers and grouse, including the Capercaillie, Black Grouse, and Ruff in northern Eurasia, and the Sage Grouse and prairie chickens in North America. These are precocial birds whose chicks leave the nest soon after they hatch and pick up their own food under maternal protection and guidance.

In the tropics, courtship assemblies are found chiefly among altricial birds, with broods of rarely more than two nestlings—in the New World, mainly hummingbirds and manakins; in the Australasian region, birds of paradise, larger and louder-voiced birds, which tend to be stationed farther apart, in expanded, or "exploded," leks.

A subtle balance of cooperation and competition prevails in a courtship assembly. Its members cooperate to establish a mating station that becomes well-known and accessible to the females in the vicinity because, the habitat remaining favorable, it is in the same place year after year, while the calls or wing sounds of the participants advertise its presence. At the same time, these males compete for females, whom they attract by vocalizations that, according to the species, may be melodious or raucous, and by visual displays that may be bizarre or enchantingly lovely. These gatherings benefit the species by providing for the females a situation in which they can readily compare the males vying for their attention and freely choose the individuals appearing most likely to sire vigorous offspring.

Incidentally, the strong intersexual selection associated with this mating system has given us many of our most beautiful birds, from dainty, glittering hummingbirds and ornate manakins and cotingas to lavishly adorned birds of paradise. Moreover, males in these assemblies appear to be safer from predation than they would be if they courted in solitude. Although the groups of performing, calling birds certainly attract attention, males would in any case need to make themselves conspicuous to be noticed by females, and by displaying in assemblies they gain the advantage of many vigilant eyes, as in flocks of all kinds. In courtship assemblies, a few dominant males, probably most often senior birds, win most of the females, while the younger members on the outskirts practice displays that may take time to perfect, becoming more successful as they grow older. Since only exceptionally do assembly members fight furiously together, they may live long.

Individuals also benefit their species by adopting young. Although not unknown among fish, mammals, and altricial birds, adoption is most frequent and spectacular among precocial birds that pick up their own food while following an adult. A parent of nidifugous chicks, who need only guidance, protection, and brooding, can attend in this manner to many more young than it can hatch; whereas parents of altricial and semialtricial young, who must be given food brought from a distance and placed in their mouths, are often unable adequately to nourish additional dependents. As they lead their families to good foraging, birds as diverse as Ostriches, rheas, grouse, sandpipers, stilts, avocets, and plovers are often joined by lost, orphaned, or abandoned chicks unrelated to them. Similarly, parent geese accumulate goslings, ducks pick up ducklings not their own. Such mixed flocks of dependents, guarded by one or a few faithful adults, can become very large, occasionally, as has been recorded of Ostriches and Shelducks, containing over one hundred young of different ages. Many nidifugous juveniles owe their lives to foster parents.

Semialtricial chicks, who leave their nests while still flightless—colonial-nesting penguins, pelicans, flamingos, and certain terns—gather in nurseries or crèches, guarded by a few adults, while their parents forage afar and bring their meals. By voice, appearance, or both, parents and young recognize each other individually; each parent feeds its own offspring, an arrangement that ensures a more equitable distribution than would result if a returning adult delivered its food to the first claimant. By this system, weak or ailing chicks, who would be pushed aside by more vigorous young if feeding were indiscriminate, are assured meals. Among nidicolous birds, a parent that has lost its mate is sometimes joined by an unattached individual of the opposite sex, who helps the bereaved parent to feed its young (Skutch 1987). Stepparents are too infrequent, or too seldom detected and reported, to affect importantly populations of abundant, strongly established species, but by even slightly increasing the reproduction of a declining species, they may help save it from extinction.

Finally, the individual dies for the good of its species. If successful in escaping all the hazards that prematurely destroy so many free animals, it grows feeble and expires from internal causes. When we recall the great recuperative power of organisms, their ability to heal wounds, recover from diseases, and restore wasted tissues, senile decay is the greatest of paradoxes. Why should animals not continue to live and reproduce indefinitely? Do they die to make room for their progeny and avoid overpopulation? It is widely held that natural selection favors the fittest or most prolific individuals: by living indefinitely, organisms might attain maximum fitness. Replacement, whether of artifacts like cars or of adult organisms, is wasteful of resources; the problem of keeping a population within the limits set by the carrying capacity of its habitat might be more economically resolved by restraining the reproduction of long-lived, if not immortal, adults, who might gain experience of value to their species.

The most probable explanation of senescence and death is that it is an evolved character, programmed by the genes. An animal is born with the seeds of its decay within it. Evolution depends upon the continuous replacement of individuals; only populations can evolve. The adaptability of individuals, limited by their heredity, may not be great enough to adjust them to changing environments. Perhaps, in the long history of the living world, species composed of potentially immortal individuals arose, only to become extinct because they lacked the flexibility that death and mutability give a species to adjust to changing conditions. Creatures die to give their species the adaptability to survive in a world of change, or to rise to higher levels of organization and mentality. After working hard to replenish its species, the individual, even in the absence of external causes, passes away, reducing by one the numerical strength of the species. Far from doing nothing for the good of its species, willingly or unwillingly the individual makes the supreme sacrifice for its species. It owes its life to the species; it relinquishes its life for the benefit of its species.

Contemporary biologists, who view all organisms as ceaselessly engaged in a relentless struggle to increase their individual fitness, as measured by the number of their progeny, use all their ingenuity to explain puzzling examples of animal behavior in ways that support their theories. They appear to delight in detecting trickery and deception in animal life. Thus, the much-discussed "beau geste" hypothesis holds that a bird sings a variety of songs in different parts of his territory to make it appear that several individuals are settled in it, thereby discouraging other males from trying to intrude. When a bird feeds nestlings or fledglings of a different species, this is a "mistake." In both of these situations, alternative explanations deserve consideration: the singer may repeat several songs because he enjoys hearing them, or because a varied repertoire, like bright plumage, makes him more attractive to females in search of a partner; the altruistic bird, well aware that the alien nestling is not its own, is moved by the youngster's pleas for food. Since we cannot read the mind of a bird, we cannot be sure which of the alternative explanations is correct; but consistently to choose the harsher interpretation makes life appear more sordid than it may actually be. Ought we not to welcome any indication among nonhuman creatures of the psychic or moral attributes that we admire in ourselves, and do our best to substantiate them? The more cooperation or kindness that we can detect in other branches of the animal kingdom, the more hopeful our own future becomes. Certainly the living world contains enough that is obviously repugnant or distressful to contemplate, without increasing its apparent amount by forced interpretations. Since, whether we like it or not, we belong to the living world, some of us wish to think well of it. Because genes impel animals to increase their own fitness, as measured by the number of their progeny, often regardless of consequences to other members of their species or to other species, they have been called "selfish."

But, as we have seen, creatures so motivated squander their strength, expose themselves to perils, and often debilitate themselves to perpetuate their species. Finally, if no accident befall them, they grow senile and die to give their species the flexibility to confront changing environments and perhaps to rise to higher levels. With the reservation that we can apply moral attributes only metaphorically to mindless molecules, should we not call genes altruistic rather than selfish?

Some of the ways that animals benefit others of their kind perplex biologists who do not look widely enough. The lineage that tried to perpetuate itself by unions of brothers and sisters or other close relatives would probably fail because of the debilitating effects of continued inbreeding. Organisms need others to provide unrelated partners for their progeny. Among the conspecifics saved by a bird's alarm cries, as among the young that it adopts, may be mates for its own descendants, or parents of such partners. Since no lineage is likely to survive long apart from a well-established species, an individual does well to promote the prosperity of its species. Paradoxically, thoughtless genes appear sometimes to see father than the clever mathematical biologists who try to interpret, in the light of their theories, behavior controlled by these genes.

3

The Twofold Nature of Animals

Life is an intensification of harmonization. A living thing, of whatever kind, contains a greater variety of components than any coherent inorganic formation of equal size, each part is more closely dependent on the others, and together they perform more diverse activities than one will find in any lifeless body of comparable extent. Because of its complexity, an organism is highly vulnerable to extremes of all sorts, and its life depends on the maintenance of a delicate balance with its surroundings. Thus it thrives only by preserving a high degree of both internal and external harmony, and where there is harmony we recognize goodness. Yet when, in chapter 1, we surveyed life broadly, trying to discover its most distinctive features and its relation to the environment that supports it, we found it aggressive and responsible for bringing evil into the world. Although violent collisions are frequent in lifeless matter, we detect there no evidence of destructive passions, malice, or the consequent frustration and suffering, which are the distinctive marks of evil as we feel it. Accordingly, it is above all in the realm of life that the universality of the impulsion toward order and harmony produces strife and evil as a secondary effect.

As products of a process that moves toward an ever more comprehensive harmony yet incidentally entangles itself in discord, living things could hardly have a perfectly consistent character. They inevitably bear the marks of the contradictions in which they are involved, displaying both good and evil qualities. We wish to know how these contrasting traits occur in them. Is there stratification, with one sort more superficial than the other, or do both penetrate to the core of animals' lives? Although consideration of their mode of origin suggests that goodness is central to living things and destructiveness more peripheral, the subject is so important that we must investigate it from another angle, trying to discover from their behavior what is the primary fact about them, and how this can be distinguished from all the accretions that mingle with and often mask it.

Contrasting Modes of Behavior

The question that now engages us will emerge in sharper outlines when we survey, even superficially, the temper and behavior of ourselves, our acquaintances, or the animals most familiar to us. All of us, people no less than other animals, are compounded of contrasting and even contradictory impulses, some so incompatible with others that, when we pause to reflect, as we too seldom do, we wonder how they could coexist in the same individual without incapacitating him or her for effective action; as two calves, tied together by a rope, each with its own notions about where the grass is sweetest, rarely wander far.

Once I had a colt who grew up in the same pasture with a gelding past his prime. From the first, the two were close companions, romping and racing together, playfully nipping each other's legs, rearing up on their hindlegs in mock battles. The old horse was always gentle with the youngster, enduring with admirable patience a surprising amount of nonsense. This friendship continued unbroken until the colt passed his fourth year and reached maturity. Then the young stallion turned against the old horse five times his age, trying to drive him from the pasture and the mares, viciously biting and kicking him if he resisted. It became necessary to keep the stallion and the gelding in separate fields, in order to preserve the peace of the farm. This altered relationship was caused wholly by changes in the stallion; the older horse remained the same and gave the younger no provocation. Which was more central to the stallion's nature, his early friendliness to the old horse or the enmity that replaced it? Or did his nature undergo a radical change as he matured, so that both the friendly and the belligerent attitudes were equally expressive of his inmost disposition at the time when each prevailed?

Among birds we witness many examples of these opposite modes of behavior. Some species that, through much of the year, associate in compact flocks lose their sociability at the approach of the nesting season, when each male establishes himself on a separate patch of land and will fight any of his erstwhile companions who dares to intrude upon it. And there is a limit to the gregariousness even of species that not only flock when not engaged in reproduction but also nest in crowded colonies on cliffs or islands or in treetops. Breeding penguins, albatrosses, and gulls repulse with their bills neighbors that press too close to their nests, with the result that each pair maintains a small unoccupied space around its nest, and this ensures a rather uniform distribution of breeding pairs over the available area. Swallows perching on wires seek one another's company yet resist too close crowding, so that neighboring individuals are separated by a distance that is determined by how far each can peck without budging from its chosen spot. Birds of many kinds feed the young of other parents, of their own or even of alien species (Skutch 1987). Yet some parent birds, including several kinds of jays and toucans, are not above snatching the young from nests of other species, perhaps bringing the mangled corpses to feed their own carefully attended families. Could we say that the social or the antagonistic instincts, the helpful or tyrannical attitudes toward neighbors, are more central to the character of a bird? Or are both equally expressive of its inmost nature?

Similar contrasts are found in the behavior of insects. Ants are among the most social of animals, dwelling in populous colonies that rival human cities in their teeming inhabitants and complex organization. The workers tenderly nurse and feed the helpless larvae, caress one another with their antennae, and pass food from mouth to mouth. Yet not only do they battle fiercely with ants of

Chinstrap Penguins, *Pygoscelis antarctica*

other species; they are almost equally hostile to other colonies of
their own kind, and they may devour the offspring of vanquished
rivals. Like humans at an early stage of moral development, they
have one pattern of behavior for their family or clan and another
for all outsiders. The two modes of behavior lie at opposite poles:
treatment of members of the clan often evinces lack of respect for
privacy and individuality that would be intolerable to cultured
people; treatment of those beyond the narrow pale of immediate
kinship reveals brutality that outrages finer feelings. Which of these
two modes of behavior, that toward one's own tribe or that toward
outsiders, is more central to the nature of ants and of men?

In trying to answer this question, we shall follow three lines of
approach. First we shall see what light the study of animal behavior
can shed upon our problem. Next we shall ask whether our understanding of evolution can help us decide which kind of behavior is
primitive and which derived. Finally, we shall try to learn whether
human experience agrees with the conclusions reached by the first
two methods of investigation. Merely as terms indicative of overt
behavior, and without reference to accompanying affective states,
we shall call all those attitudes and activities that tend to draw
animals together "friendly" or "integrative," all those that make
them avoid or harm each other "hostile" or "disruptive."

HUNGER AND FEAR AS CAUSES OF HOSTILITY

The chief causes of conflict among animals are hunger and sexual rivalry. The need or inclination of each individual or closely knit group, in many species, to preserve for itself, and keep free from others of its kind, a territory or area that provides food or shelter or both is a secondary cause of conflict: the defended space would have little value if it failed to yield nourishment or to hold rivals aloof. On the whole, sexual rivalry is not a major cause of avoidance or fear among animals; much of the so-called sexual fighting, especially in birds, is formal jousting that rarely results in injury to either contestant. As a rule, the victor in these duels has no incentive to pursue his fleeing antagonist beyond his own domain; and when the season of resproduction has passed, the former rivals may gather in friendly groups once more. This leaves hunger as the great disruptive force in the animal world, the chief cause of fear. Because some animals need others as food, these others must defend themselves desperately or else flee for their lives. Unlike an animal withdrawing from a sexual rival, who is usually satisfied by the departure of his antagonist, the creature fleeing from a predator can satisfy its pursuer only with its living flesh.

Aside from humans and some of the social hymenoptera, animals rarely wage war or kill other animals except to fill their stomachs. When not hungry, predatory animals, including some of the fiercest, only exceptionally molest others, even of kinds on which they habitually prey. Antelopes and other herbivores are somehow able to recognize the moods or intentions of the carnivores that eat them, galloping away from hunting lions but continuing to graze peacefully in the vicinity of these hereditary enemies when the latter are not interested in prey. Similarly, ducks have been seen swimming about fearlessly while carnivorous otters played among them. Hawks that catch smaller birds often hunt chiefly at a distance from their nests, leaving unmolested small songbirds rearing broods beneath the eyrie. The birds learn which kinds of hawks are dangerous and which relatively innocuous, and they may sometimes be seen feeding calmly in the tree where one of the latter sort rests.

Some animals instinctively avoid predators that have for generations preyed upon their kind, but they lack an innate tendency to shun other animals in general; so that they may remain unconcerned near one so potentially dangerous as man, until disastrous encounters, over a long interval, have taught a sort of wisdom to their race. Thus, it is well-known that birds and other creatures on uninhabited islands, or in other regions from which humans had long been absent, proved fearless of people, with the lamentable consequence that mariners who encountered them in their pristine innocence exterminated whole species before they acquired wariness, as happened to the Great Auk of Labrador and the Dodo of Mauritius.

Moreover, even among the predators themselves, the habit of capturing and tearing the prey appears in some instances to be not innate but learned from the example of parents or others of their kind. We learn from Lockwood Kipling's *Beast and Man in India* (1892) that the young Cheetah is not worth catching, for it has not learned to hunt and its human captors cannot teach it. Konrad Lorenz (1952), the famous student of animal behavior, owned a female Imperial Eagle, acquired after she was already mature. Even when hungry she refused to harm a hair of the rabbit offered to her. Facts such as these, which might be multiplied, suggest that neither the predator's fierceness nor the timid hunted creature's shyness is an expression of its essential or inmost nature. These contrasting attitudes arose because they were needed for survival; when the need is satisfied or removed, the conduct and the accompanying emotions vanish. This conclusion was reached by the ancients: in his essay on abstinence from flesh, Porphyry quoted with approval Aristotle's statement that if all animals enjoyed abundant food, they would not act ferociously toward each other or toward humans.

What remains in the animal when these disruptive tendencies have been neutralized or eradicated? Either indifference to creatures of other kinds or a measure of positive attraction. Social or gregarious animals are, as a rule, little drawn to animals of other species as long as they can find comrades of their own kind, but in the absence of these they may seek heterogeneous companions. A solitary horse at pasture stays nearer his master than does one with equine friends. Some kinds of birds that, even outside the nesting season, retain too much territorial exclusiveness to associate with others of their kind nevertheless attach themselves to mixed parties of distinct species, one individual of the exclusive species in each flock, as though preferring some companionship to a wholly solitary life. The pretty Slate-throated Redstart of the Guatemalan highlands is a good example of such behavior.

Under domestication, when people have brought together creatures of diverse sorts with little regard for their natural affinities, the most incongruous companionships may grow up between individuals deprived of access to others of their kind. Domestic horses have contracted friendships with a swan and a hen, and wild mustangs with bison. Dogs have accepted as comrades a variety of animals that they usually persecute, including a deer, a peccary, an otter, a lioness, rabbits, and squirrels. Crows can be trained to dwell peacefully with owls. These are a few of the strange companionships that naturalists have recorded (Dobie 1945).

Just as evolution has covered certain animals with hard carapaces or sharp quills to protect their tender flesh, so it has overlaid their basically pacific nature with fierceness, to help them survive in a fiercely competitive world. But the fierce temper is as superficial as the protective integument. Hereditary enmity, the normal relationship between predator and prey, tends to disappear if individuals of both categories are reared together soon after birth, before one has learned to kill and the other to fear, and if enough food is provided for both. Even animals as fierce and powerful as lions, leopards, bears, and wolves will grow up as affectionate friends of the person who attends them gently from an early age. Perhaps only animals of very low intelligence, which seize their prey by a reflex act little subject to inhibition by the higher nervous centers, are intrinsically incapable of becoming trustworthy companions. Without the ferocity fomented by hunger, and the timidity of victims of predation, the whole animal kingdom might become the pacific community that Isaiah envisioned.

SEXUAL RIVALRY

The second great source of strife in the animal kingdom is sexual rivalry. Whereas hunger brings discord between different species and is far less a direct cause of conflict between animals of the same kind, the reverse is true of the enmity stirred up by the reproductive passions. This is displayed almost exclusively between individuals of the same species and sex, usually between males, although in a few kinds of birds in which the usual roles of the sexes in courtship and parental care are reversed, as in the phalaropes, jacanas, and Spotted Sandpiper, the female is more aggressive than the male. Among vertebrates, sexual jealousy does not, as a rule, arise until the animal approaches reproductive maturity, and in nearly all species in a state of nature it is intermittent, occurring only in the season of rutting or mating. Gregarious birds and mammals of the male sex, having grown up peacefully together in flocks or herds, become antagonistic to their former companions and playmates as they mature. At this stage the males of numerous monogamous species separate. Each claims a territory that he defends against others of his sex, while he uses all his arts to attract a mate. Polygamous males may fight stubbornly to drive away all competitors and each become the sole master of a harem. But after the close of the breeding season, these same rivals may reunite in a peaceful group.

This strenuous sexual rivalry is induced largely by hormones that the reproductive organs release into the bloodstream at the period of their greatest development and activity. It has long been known that geldings and oxen graze pacifically together while stallions and bulls brook no rivals. Castrated pigeons and other birds remain tranquilly with their male companions at seasons when they would normally fight. Conversely, by injections of appropriate hormones, quails can be made pugnacious in the winter months when otherwise they would be foraging in amicable flocks. Here, too, the basic and primary state of the animal is pacific and sociable. Sexual jealousy, with all the exclusiveness and sometimes fierce belligerency that accompany it, results from the modification of this prevailing condition by a chemical poured into the blood-stream and acting upon the nervous system, thereby inducing distinctive attitudes and modes of behavior. There are reasons for believing that this whole arrangement was brought about by natural selection, because of the advantages that accrue to a species in a world of conflict when the strongest males win more mates and leave more progeny than the weaker ones, or when the breeding individuals are scattered rather than crowded together.

In many species, the male reproductive apparatus is a Nessus' shirt that diffuses a subtle poison through the unfortunate animal, destroying his amiable tranquillity and bringing on a sort of mad-ness. The hormones it releases have much the same effect as a blow in the face of a peaceful man, who doubles up his fits to strike back almost before he is aware of what he is doing. The effects of anger, as of fear, are intensified by a hormone that quickens circu-lation, deepens breathing, and tenses muscles. But no special hormone is needed to make animals placid and sociable. This is their primary state, which may be masked by the goading of hunger or the disquieting secretions of the sexual glands but can hardly be permanently altered without destroying their health or sanity. Yet even in this upsetting matter of sexual jealously, life's integrative force has asserted itself, turning rivals into associates and making of competition a mode of cooperation, as in the court-ship assemblies of male birds mentioned in chapter 4.

HOW STRIFE ENTERED THE LIVING WORLD

Our survey of some of the pertinent facts of animal behavior suggests that friendly or integrative attitudes are more fundamental or central, closer to the basic, unmodified character of animal life, than are hostile or disruptive attitudes. When we reflect upon the origin of organisms, we see that it could hardly be otherwise. Life arose as a late phase in a long course of harmonization, which is, above all, the process of building up coherent patterns. Life could not flourish on this planet until cosmic and terrestrial developments had prepared a fairly stable, orderly environment for it. First, diffuse nebular material condensed into definite, widely separated bodies, moving rhythmically in dynamic equilibrium with distant neighbors. Then on the cooling surface of Earth the mixed vapors separated out, forming the atmosphere and the oceans, with emergent areas of land. The peculiar properties of air and water and the regular diurnal rotation of the sphere stabilized the temperature within limits compatible with vital processes. Only in such a moderate milieu, shielded alike from extremes of heat and cold, of radiation and chemical activity, could the integrative process that is life be carried forward. Then atoms could unite in molecules of extraordinary complexity, and these join in colloidal masses, which encased themselves in delicate membranes that regulated their exchanges of materials with the environing world.

As evolution proceeded, the primitive cells, instead of separating into independent halves after each fission induced by their increasing size, remained in contact and gave rise to multicellular organisms. As these aggregates of cells grew in bulk, those on the outside were exposed to conditions different from those near the center, and this diversity of situation induced differences in structure and function. Distinguishable tissues arose in these early organisms, and with continuing evolution diverse tissues were grouped into distinct organs. Eventually, animals and plants were equipped with a great diversity of organs, external and internal, each with its own marvelously complex structure and its particular function in the economy of the whole organism. To ensure the proper coordination of these separate organs and functions, each so necessary to the welfare of the whole body, integrative devices developed in the form of the nervous system and an array of chemical messengers which, released into the circulatory system by one organ, effected correlative modifications in others, often widely separated from the first. And while this internal development was proceeding, the whole cellular community remained sensitively responsive to modifications in its surroundings, for its prosperity depended, above all, on close adjustment to the environment that sustained it.

Thus, life could not appear until it found a fairly stable environment. From first to last, its evolution has depended upon harmonization, not only for the close integration of an increasing multiplicity of parts but likewise for adjusting this manifold to its ambience. Life arose out of harmony; it is a constant endeavor to preserve and increase harmony; it languishes or perishes with the failure of harmony, either in its internal arrangements or in its relations with its milieu. How, then, did this tender and delicate thing, this triumph of harmonization, ever become capable of violence?

Strife arose from the collision of patterns growing up at separate centers and incapable of coalescing into a single whole. Such fusion was impeded by the integument in which each living unit found it expedient to enclose itself in order to carry on its intricate processes without much interference from outside. Moreover, the complex molecules of the living substance, although exhibiting a fundamental similarity in chemical constitution, soon acquired different structures in diverse organisms, so that the simple fusion of distinct masses of protoplasm was no longer possible. The great profusion of life, the tendency to initiate these patterns of superior complexity and integration everywhere on Earth's surface that they could exist, inevitably resulted in the clash of living things, which is but a special instance of the general truth that the excessive intensity of the impulsion toward harmony gives birth to disharmony.

Increase in the number of organisms not only resulted in more frequent physical contacts between them; so many living things absorbing nutrients impoverished the medium and made the maintenance of life more difficult. Conditions were approaching an impasse that might have blocked the evolution of life had it not been broken. Finally, some of the primitive organisms developed the capacity to break down the substance of other organisms, take it into their bodies, and incorporate it into their own protoplasm. Possibly at first they used only dead organisms in this way; but since many of the protista multiply by simple fission and probably never die of old age, lifeless protoplasm might have been available only where the excessive heat or insolation of some exposed pool had destroyed its inhabitants; or where overcrowding of these minute creatures potentially endowed with immortality caused many to perish from malnutrition, thereby releasing for the hardiest and most adaptable survivors the materials they needed to preserve life.

Whether or not the earliest organisms that nourished themselves on other organisms consumed only dead ones, it is certain that eventually living things began to prey on one another. This prepared the way for a tremendously long and intricate evolution in two complementary directions. In the first place, the organisms most helpless in the face of the primitive predators would be devoured in greatest numbers; while those that could move away, or were protected by a resistant envelope or a peculiar chemical composition that made them unacceptable to their enemies, survived and multiplied. Every character that increased the security of victims of predation acquired survival value; mutations improving such features had still greater survival value; and lineages in which existence depended upon swift retreat, or concealment, or protective incrustations, or a fecundity able to compensate for high mortality started down the long evolutionary road. As the victims of predation became more adept at avoiding capture, the predators simultaneously increased their speed or craft or strength for overcoming their prey, for those best endowed in any of these ways were most adequately nourished and, on the whole, left more descendants. Another category of animals, specialized for predation, began to evolve, producing by adaptive radiation an ever-increasing array of types, and keeping pace with the prey, which by developing fresh modes of defense or escape fled them down the geologic ages.

STRIFE INTRUDES INTO REPRODUCTIVE ACTIVITIES

At first, simple reactions sufficed for predatory animals to capture victims that possessed only equally stereotyped reactions for escaping. But with the increasing size and structural complexity of both predators and prey, more complex innate patterns of behavior were impressed upon their nervous systems, on the one hand promoting the capture of victims and on the other, escape from the pursuing predator. Concomitant with the evolution of the nervous system was an intensification of psychic life, which necessarily corresponded with each animal's mode of existence. Predators became bold and fierce, especially when pricked by the pangs of hunger; creatures whose safety lay in flight or concealment became timid and secretive. Intelligence, slowly increasing to give greater plasticity to the behavior of certain gifted animals, was at first almost wholly under the dominance of those appetites and emotions essential to the survival of the individual and its race, so that its mind was swayed by greed, rage, and anger, or by fear, hatred, and suspicion.

With the growth of the carnivorous habit among animals, death crept over Earth in countless guises, and to compensate for its ravages, the multiplication of individuals became urgent. Animals with many diverse parts could not, like their most primitive ancestors, multiply by simple fission, and more complex modes of reproduction became indispensable. Instead of giving its whole self to produce two replicas of itself, in the manner of the humblest organisms, the multicellular creature set apart a fraction of its body to generate several or many offspring at first wholly different in appearance from itself. Instead of a single individual's sufficing to propagate its kind, the cooperation of two individuals became necessary throughout the metazoa, the reason for this complex arrangement being that, by mingling the traits of individuals, a greater variety of offspring is produced, some displaying new characters or combinations of characters that bring advantages in the increasingly intense struggle to survive.

The cooperation of two individuals in reproduction demands a high degree of harmony between them. Their external genitalia must be complementary; their physiological cycles must be so adjusted that they are simultaneously ready to mate; their patterns of behavior must be coordinated; their germinal cells must have mutual affinity so that they fuse; and their genetic constitutions must be such that when combined they produce a well-integrated organism. If the two parents remain together after the fertilization of the ova and cooperate to rear the young, their interactions with each other and with their developing progeny must be closely adjusted. At least at higher psychic levels, this intricate process is colored by appropriate emotions, the chief of which, love, is the most powerful agent of concord among individuals. The whole reproductive process, in its physical no less than in its psychic aspects, is a masterpiece of harmonization in the living world.

The intrusion of disruptive, hostile passions and behavior into this realm of subtle and delicate adjustments is one of the great paradoxes of animal life, explicable only when we understand how sexual rivalry is related to the deadlier conflict between predator and prey. The strife stirred up by the carnivorous habit finally insinuated itself into the intimate internal relations of each affected species, whether of predatory animals or their victims. Among the former, any system that would make the strongest and most pugnacious males most successful in winning mates and fathering offspring would help the race to attain maximum efficiency in running down and overpowering its prey. Among the latter, the selection of the hardiest and boldest males as sires would result in progeny better able to escape their pursuers by sustained flight or even to confront them when the presence of defenseless young made retreat inexpedient.

Accordingly, natural selection promoted the fierce competition among the males of many mammals and other animals that tends to deprive the weaker or less enduring individuals of a share in reproducing their kind, while the more powerful ones pass on their size and vigor to the next generation. And this fighting, as Darwin recognized, led indirectly to the origination or further development both of horns, antlers, tusks, claws, spurs, and other offensive weapons and of tough skin, carapaces, capes of feathers, manes, and other protective coverings, no less than to the increase of sheer bulk, strength, and endurance in the contestants. Much of this offensive and defensive armament helps the animals that wear it, in their encounters with hereditary enemies as well as in duels with rivals of their own kind. But perhaps the energy and determination needed for the effective use of this equipment in intrasexual struggles is, in the long run, of greater value to the species than the often clumsy and bizarre excrescences themselves. Thus, the strife between predator and prey abetted sexual fighting, which by selecting the victors to become parents made this strife ever more savage.

By so long and devious a path has the impulsion toward harmony of which life is a product become entangled in antagonistic habits and attitudes, been armed with a vast array of aggressive and protective devices; until, regarding the living world superficially, one might suppose that discord rather than concord, war rather than peace, is its fundamental character and prime necessity. But an intimate study of its origin and nature reveals that this conclusion is false. Disharmony can never be more than froth upon the deep current of life. A system of relations so extensive and intricate remains intact solely by virtue of the harmony that pervades it; to saturate it with strife is to ensure its dissolution. In structures, in functions, in emotions, harmony is the pulsating heart of life; discord, the armor its puts on to confront the world. And from this discord, growing out of the physical problems of life, moral evil at last arose when, after millions of years of slow evolution, humankind became capable of foreseeing the future and choosing between alternative courses of action.

A Diagram of Animal Nature

For clarity and brevity, the conclusions reached in this chapter are summarized in the accompanying diagram, which includes ourselves, who share so many attributes with animals and in whom some of the tendencies of animal life reach their most revealing expressions. At the center of the diagram is the primary nature of organisms, which in humans has been called the central self. A product of life's formative agent, harmonization, the expression of which in living things is growth, this primary nature is the same in all of them, plants as well as animals, and is everywhere creative and pacific. This is most clearly evident in green plants able to synthesize their own food from elements present in air, water, and soil, an achievement that exempts them from the necessity to

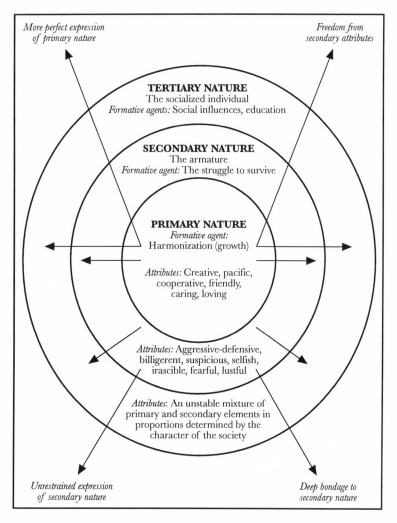

More perfect expression
of primary nature

Freedom from
secondary attributes

TERTIARY NATURE
The socialized individual
Formative agents: Social influences, education

SECONDARY NATURE
The armature
Formative agent: The struggle to survive

PRIMARY NATURE
Formative agent:
Harmonization (growth)

Attributes: Creative, pacific,
cooperative, friendly,
caring, loving

Attributes: Aggressive-defensive,
billigerent, suspicious, selfish,
irascible, fearful, lustful

Attributes: An unstable mixture of
primary and secondary elements in
proportions determined by the
character of the society

Unrestrained expression
of secondary nature

Deep bondage to
secondary nature

A DIAGRAM OF ANIMAL NATURE
(including humans)

The central circle represents the primary nature of all animals, including humans. This is surrounded by a ring representing their secondary nature, which in turn is enclosed by a ring representing their tertiary or socialized nature. At the bottom of the circle and each of the rings are some of the attributes corresponding to each nature, most of which will be manifest only at higher psychic levels. Arrows pointing outward indicate that elements from one sphere enter enclosing spheres, modifying their character; or they transcend the external ring, as when the pacific primary nature rises above a belligerent society, or when, at the opposite extreme, the aggressiveness of the secondary nature escapes social restraints to make outlaws.

exploit other creatures. The primary nature of the higher animals is expressed by friendly or loving attitudes, cooperation, caring, and creating. Animals start with a handicap. Unable to synthesize their own food, they must exploit other living things and often struggle stubbornly with them to survive. This conflict has developed their secondary nature, which surrounds their primary nature like an armature and is represented by a ring around the central circle. Their secondary nature is, in varying degrees in different species and individuals, aggressive-defensive, belligerent, suspicious, selfish, irascible, fearful, and lustful.

Animals in which the secondary nature is highly developed and untamed are unfit for social life. To live in societies, this rude secondary nature must be mitigated, suppressed, or somehow controlled, so that elements of the primary nature may break through it—the process of socialization. Many animals appear to have become innately socialized as their societies evolved, but a measure of training or the example of their elders may be needed to finish the process. Ornithologists have noticed that Florida Scrub jays, Arabian Babblers, and Jungle Babblers of India, often disorderly and quarrelsome when young, become as they mature well-behaved members of their pacific cooperative breeding groups. Young humans are socialized by discipline, example, and education during their prolonged immaturity. The result of this process is the tertiary nature of social animals, represented by a ring around the secondary nature. The attributes of this tertiary nature are an unstable mixture of primary and secondary elements, in proportions determined by the innate quality of the individual and the character of its society.

The rings around the primary nature are not impenetrable barriers. In socialization, attributes of the primary nature penetrate the secondary nature to become manifest in the tertiary nature, as is indicated by arrows extending from the central circle to the outer ring. Occasionally in other social animals, and all too frequently in people, attributes of the secondary nature break through the social restraints, as is suggested by arrows passing from the armature to below the outermost circle. When this happens, animals become aggressive and destructive members of their societies; humans become dangerous criminals, often of the lowest cast, or dominating their society, cruel, oppressive tyrants.

As we know only too well, our actual societies are not the harmonious associations of friendly, cooperative people that we long for them to be. Our treatment of the natural world that supports us threatens to wreck it; we abuse and needlessly slaughter beautiful, harmless animals that deserve our protection. People whose primary nature burns strongly within them, perhaps thinly overlaid by their secondary nature, yearn to transcend the narrowness of their societies. They wish to live in harmony with all creatures, not only their fellow citizens. In their efforts to achieve this more inclusive harmony, they may adopt habits that cause them to be mocked, avoided, or persecuted. They rise above the conventional level of their society, often to lonely heights, as indicated by arrows passing from the central circle through both enclosing rings to rise above the outermost.

The diagram corroborates the judgment of philosophers who long ago proclaimed that human nature, despite its manifold blemishes, is intrinsically good. The Socratic doctrine that people naturally seek the good but mistake it, hence can be made virtuous by teaching them to judge correctly, is recognition of humanity's basic goodness. Far away in China, the sage Mencius (1942), who can hardly have been influenced by the Athenian philosopher, compared human nature to a mountain that had been wooded with beautiful trees, which were ruthlessly felled to supply timber to a neighboring city, leaving desolate slopes where every aspiring shoot was cropped by cows and goats. Similarly, the benevolence and moral rectitude that are our natural endowment are weakened by our daily toil. Mencius could not have known for how long an age, under what harsh conditions, evolution had been weaving an aggressive-defensive armature that tends to mask the central goodness of people and other animals.

As sages have long recognized, obsession by the disturbing passions of this armature is human bondage; emancipation from their oppressive dominance is freedom and mental tranquillity.

When the motivation of our acts springs from our primary nature, uninfluenced by secondary accretions, we consistently choose the course that best promotes harmony, as far as we can foresee the consequences of actions. Our will is free, not by virtue of some nebulous indeterminacy but because it is an expression of the true and inmost self; and who can be freer than one whose course is determined by the process that formed and sustains one's body, gives coherence to one's thoughts and benevolence to one's will?

4

Mutual Aid and Social Relations

To emphasize the vast disproportion between the number of plants and animals of all kinds that nature produces and the number that can survive to reproduce, and the resulting severe competition between individuals of the same species no less than between those of different species, was essential to the argument of Darwin's *The Origin of Species by Means of Natural Selection*. Evolutionary change depended upon the survival, in this ceaseless struggle, of those best fitted to survive. To Darwinists of the latter part of the nineteenth century, nature was "red in tooth and claw," a monster proclaiming, "I care for nothing, all shall go," But it would be unjust to hold Darwin solely responsible for the prevalence of this attitude. The famous phrases quoted were written by Tennyson between 1833 and 1849 and published in 1850, nine years before the appearance of Darwin's great work.

Obsessed by the idea that relentless struggle is indispensable for evolutionary advance, the Social Darwinists advocated a competitive society, with few props for the weak and the faltering. They seemed to forget that the attributes most promoting survival and reproduction in a fiercely competitive system are not those which raise humans above the level of the shark and the tiger. Fitness to survive and fitness to live in a society of which spiritually awakened people can be proud are two quite different things.

Although from Darwin's later writings, especially *The Descent of Man and Selection in Relation to Sex*, it is clear that he recognized that cooperation influences the course of evolution no less than does competition, particularly in humans; it remained for others to demonstrate how widespread is cooperation in the living world. Perhaps no one did more to promote a more balanced attitude toward evolution, at least among English-speaking people, than Prince Piotr Alexeivich Kropotkin, a Russian nobleman and anarchist long resident in England, who in 1902 published *Mutual Aid: A Factor in Evolution*, the chapters of which had appeared in the preceding decade in the *Nineteenth Century*.

Kropotkin's work has been condemned as uncritical. At the time he wrote, scarcely any of the patient, systematic, critical field studies of free animals, studies now available in increasing numbers, had been made; he had, perforce, to select most of his examples of mutual aid in the animal world from incidental observations, especially those of travelers and huntsmen. But his approach was essentially sound; and no one can justly accuse him of a one-sided attitude or of failure to recognize the prevalence of conflict in nature. "Rousseau," he wrote, "had committed the error of excluding the beak-and-claw fight from his thoughts; and Huxley committed the opposite error; but neither Rousseau's optimism nor Huxley's pessimism can be accepted as an impartial interpretation of nature." Kropotkin believed that animals associate together not only for the security that numbers give but to increase their enjoyment of life; he surmised that birds often fly in flocks "for the mere pleasure of the flight." Modern biologists are inclined to scorn such notions as unscientific, and to account for all animal associations by their purely utilitarian function of promoting survival and reproduction; but unless creatures find some satisfaction or joy in living, and this increases along with advancing organization, evolution—which multiplies their kinds and elevates their organization—is futility on a stupendous scale, signifying nothing.

More recently, W. C. Allee (1951), long of the University of Chicago, explored cooperation in nature, performing with his students many carefully controlled laboratory experiments to demonstrate that organisms in groups help one another to survive. He proved that animals, such as goldfish in a tank poisoned with colloidal silver, planarian worms exposed to ultraviolet radiation, or marine worms transferred to fresh water, buffer one another from adverse effects and survive longer if exposed to hazards in groups rather than singly. Sea urchin eggs develop more rapidly when crowded than when scattered; and certain bacteria fail to multiply if too few are inoculated into the culture medium. Accordingly, Allee recognized an "unconscious proto-cooperation" among organisms low on the evolutionary scale and traced its growth into the more advanced cooperation of higher animals. He recognized that for many organisms there is an optimum concentration, neither too sparse nor too crowded, that most promotes vital processes.

In the natural as in the human world, cooperation and competition are so intimately intertwined that it is often difficult to disentangle them. I am impressed with this truth as, through my study window, I gaze out upon the forest dripping from October's torrential rains. The dominant trees in this rain forest compete intensely for a place in the sunlit canopy, where alone some species can flower and set seed freely. Probably not one in ten thousand seedlings succeeds, after many years of patient growth, in thrusting itself up into this privileged position, for which it must often wait until the giant beneath which it germinated dies of old age or falls in a windstorm. Yet these trees, bewildering in variety, that compete so strenuously, create the conditions indispensable for one another's growth.

One might suppose that trees finding competition in the forest so severe would be the first to take advantage of a clearing that men had made in or adjoining the forest and had abandoned after taking off a crop or two; their seeds are often carried to such clearings by birds, bats, terrestrial animals, or wind. But nothing of the sort happens; the trees that invade the new clearings are nearly all of different, fast-growing species that are rare in the forest, where they occur chiefly in openings made by the fall of a great tree. Only after the second-growth trees have profoundly changed conditions in the clearing do the true forest trees invade it; many years, probably centuries, must pass before the original forest is reconstituted.

The forest trees not only compete with one another; they cooperate to create a favorable environment for themselves and all the lesser creatures that depend on them.

About the edges of this same forest over which I look, I find the courtship assemblies of male Orange-collared Manakins. These tiny, brisk birds compete pacifically for the females of their kind, who come to have their developing eggs fertilized. One might assume that each manakin's chances of winning a temporary partner would be better if he established his courtship station at a distance from his rivals, instead of within hearing, and often also within sight, of a number of them. But apparently this is not true, for perhaps the majority of the avian species that follow this mating system display in groups or assemblies rather than in isolation. They cooperate to establish an assembly that persists in the same locality year after year, and is large and conspicuous enough to be easily found by the females, at the same time that they vie intensely to attract the females visiting the assembly (Skutch 1992).

Examples of a similar mixture of cooperation and competition among humans are not hard to find. In a big city, shops that sell similar goods are often located close together on the same street or in the same section. Although they compete for customers, they likewise help one another by making it widely known that this is the part of the town where shoes, or jewelry, or whatever one wants, is to be found. In both nature and human society, opposites such as cooperation and competition, good and evil, beauty and ugliness, are so intricately intermixed that we must be wary of all sweeping generalizations.

MUTUAL PROTECTION

One of the most widespread forms of mutual aid in the animal kingdom is cooperation in escaping enemies. Everywhere the milder birds and mammals appear to have formed defensive alliances to protect themselves from the fierce predators. When they spy an approaching hawk, birds give special cries, often loud and sharp, that cause others to fall silent and dive into the nearest available cover—not only other individuals of their own species but likewise birds of other kinds, so that a hush falls over fields and groves as the raptor sails by.

Mammals and birds reciprocally warn each other of perils. While intensively studying Mule Deer in the Sierra Nevada of California, Thane Riney (1951) often saw the deer alerted to the approach of a person or some other dangerous animal by the alarm notes of birds that had noticed the intruder first. The birds, of several kinds, not only warned the quadrupeds of peril; by resuming their songs or other activities, they reassured the deer that the danger had passed, so that the latter returned to their grazing or undisturbed repose. By imitating appropriate notes of the birds, Riney could not only alert the deer but also allay their fears.

On the African savannas, Ostriches often associate with antelopes and other herbivorous animals. Because they are taller than most of the associated quadrupeds and have sharper eyesight, the birds often warn their four-footed companions of impending danger. It is probable, too, that they profit by the mammals' keener sense of smell, when the approaching predator is not in sight or tries to steal up under cover of darkness. Once, while I stood watching a covey of Marbled Wood-Quails in a banana plantation, a squirrel in the crown of a nearby banana plant noticed me and scolded sharply. Although the birds could not have been unaware that I had been standing close to them, on hearing the rodent, four of them instantly squatted down on the ground in plain view, while the fifth ran behind a clump of bananas. I remained motionless, and soon the quails resumed feeding close in front of me.

At the sight of a flying hawk, the gregarious California Ground Squirrel utters a loud *cheesk*, which is repeated by neighboring squirrels as each slips into its hole. A series of different notes warns the community of the presence of a snake; and yet another call advises neighbors that a person, a dog, or a coyote is approaching (Bourlière 1954).

Many kinds of animals find safety in numbers. At the approach of a Peregrine Falcon, European Starlings, flying in a flock, bunch more compactly and make sudden, closely coordinated turns. A falcon dashing into such a dense flock at tremendous speed would injure itself by colliding with some of the starlings, hence will try to seize only an isolated individual (Tinbergen 1951). Similarly, a flock of Cedar Waxwings, repeatedly menaced by a Cooper's Hawk, contracted into a dense mass and veered aside in unison each time the raptor tried to seize one of them, always failing (Meyerriecks 1957). The November 1988 issue of *National Geographic* includes an underwater photograph by David Doubilet of a school of Crevalle Jackfish swimming in close contact while they chased a great barracuda that they had thwarted when it attacked them. On the ground, in the air, and under the water, gregarious animals employ similar methods to baffle their enemies.

The caterpillars of several kinds of butterflies live in clusters, sometimes dozens or hundreds of them forming a conspicuous, compact sheet on the bark of a tree. Since at least some kinds of these gregarious caterpillars are palatable to birds, one might suppose that to make themselves so visible would be disastrous. But it has been demonstrated in the case of the Small Tortoiseshell and the Peacock that certain birds, such as redstarts, hesitate to attack the caterpillars while clustering, although they devour one of the same kind if they find it alone. Why the birds avoid clustered harmless caterpillars I do not know.

In other ways, too, the massing together of small creatures may give them a measure of safety. Midges flitting back and forth in a dense aggregation or crowded tiny animals darting at random in the water may be harder to catch than if they were more thinly dispersed. A predator closely pursuing one of them seems to be thrown off the track by another suddenly crossing its path. Allee, who noticed that goldfish ate fewer rather than more *Daphnia* when these small crustaceans were very crowded in the water, called this the "confusion effect."

From ancient times, it has been known that an owl drowsing on an exposed perch in the daytime is often surrounded by a crowd of small birds of the most varied kinds, all flitting closely around the sleepy raptor and calling in a medley of voices. The Greeks, as we learn from a remark in the Olympian discourse of Dio Chrysostom, supposed that the birds were admiring the owl; but the modern explanation is different. Similar behavior, known as "mobbing," is elicited by a perching hawk, a snake, a cat, and indeed any animal dangerous to small birds or their nests. Attracted by the hubbub, I have sometimes found nothing more formidable than a very large, moribund moth at the center of the crowd of excited birds. The birds scarcely ever touch the creature that they mob; but I have known Riverside Wrens and Rufous-fronted Thornbirds to peck snakes a dozen times their own length, always being careful to keep away from the serpent's head. Mobbing serves to warn every small animal in the vicinity that a potential enemy is present. It is always a great advantage to know exactly where one's enemies are; not the snake that is seen but the snake that escapes detection sinks its venomous fangs into the unwary pedestrian's leg. Moreover, by joining a group of mobbers, young birds learn which animals are dangerous.

Some animals give a warning sound, or flash a warning signal, as they flee from an actual or potential enemy. Pigeons sometimes clap their wings loudly as they take flight, thereby alerting other pigeons. Hares thump the ground with their feet. The Agouti, a large nearly tailless terrestrial rodent of tropical American forests, emits a startlingly loud note, like a harsh sneeze, as it bounds away from an approaching person Although the Agouti is a solitary animal, the only evident function of their revealing cry is to warn other Agoutis in the surrounding woodland; if it fled silently, the animal would more often escape detection and death.

The white caudal flags that White-tailed Deer and Cottontail Rabbits flaunt so conspicuously as they bound away seem also to serve as warning signals to others of their kind; the animals' own safety might be better served if they held their tails down, rather than up, as they flee. More complex is the warning behavior of the African Springbuck. Along the posterior half of the back of this antelope is a double fold of skin forming a narrow pouch lined with pure white hairs from four to six inches long. When alarmed, springbucks leap high into the air with body curved, legs close together, and head down. At the same time, the pouch is everted, displaying the long white hairs like a fan over the rump.

SOCIAL HIERARCHIES

Since the Norwegian T. Schjelderup-Ebbe published his study of the social psychology of the domestic hen in 1922, much has been written, in "popular" no less than scientific publications, about social dominance and despotism among animals, including humans. In certain flocks and herds, all or most of the individuals are arranged in a hierarchy of power or privilege. In hens, social rank is revealed by the peck order. The top hen pecks all the others but is pecked by none. The second hen is pecked only by the first, and she pecks all the others except the first. The third hen pecks all except the first and second, and so on, down to the most subordinate hen, who is liable to be pecked by all her associates in the flock but is too timid to retaliate. At times a triangle develops somewhere in such a series, A pecking B, who pecks C, who in turn pecks A. Anyone who has tried to put a hand beneath one of the more peppery hens while she incubates or broods her young knows that a hen's peck can be painful.

The situation among hens is known as "peck right." In domestic pigeons it is more complex and known as "peck dominance." The pigeon that is pecked does not always tamely submit to this aggression but often returns what it receives. To discover the hierarchy in a flock of pigeons requires long, patient watching and counting of the pecks delivered in all directions. A bird who pecks another more than it is pecked by that other is considered to be dominant over the other.

Social hierarchies have been demonstrated in animals the most diverse, including fish and lizards, gregarious quadrupeds, monkeys, and humans. Among cows, the dominant animal butts her subordinates with her horns; among humans, as everyone knows, social dominance is shown in the most varied ways, blunt or subtle, and often no less hurtful than a hen's peck or a cow's butt.

The position of an animal in a social hierarchy depends on various factors, some of which are obscure. Age and experience are certainly of the greatest importance; the youngest members of any group generally stand at the bottom of the ladder and must gradually work their way upward, suffering many harsh rebuffs on the way. Strength and vigor count for much, but temperament is equally decisive; a large but mild animal may yield to a smaller, more aggressive companion. Intelligence may also help to win a high rank. A high-ranking animal that becomes sick or suffers an injury may fall from the top to the bottom of the hierarchy. A newcomer in a flock or herd, timid amid strange companions and unfamiliar surroundings, usually enters it with a low rank; but if a strong or aggressive bird or mammal, it may soon fight or bluff its way upward.

Sex also influences social rank, but in no invariable fashion. In Budgerigars, or Shell Parakeets, females are dominant over males when they are not nesting; but while breeding is in progress, the males dominate their mates and are said to drive them back to their eggs when they attempt to leave. In the European Jay and the Canary, however, the situation is just the reverse: the male of a pair is dominant over his mate in the off season; but as nesting begins, she assumes the ascendancy (Shoemaker 1939). In some birds, such as the Jackdaws that Konrad Lorenz (1952) kept at Altenberg, the female, whatever her original rank, acquires that of the daw with whom she mates, so that a low-ranking female may suddenly find herself at the top if she wins the leading male. The diligent reader of history will doubtless recall parallel cases among people.

Some naturalists have contended that for successful coition the male must win dominance over the female, but this fallacy appears to result from the confusion of spatial position with personality or social standing. It would be as logical to maintain that the motorcar is dominant over the mechanic who crawls beneath to repair it. Not infrequently, as I have seen in woodpeckers and as has been reported in other birds, male and female alternately mount each other. Sometimes the male of a pair is the stronger character, sometimes the female; and I have watched many a pair of birds build and attend their nests without any indication that either lorded it over the other.

Dominance in a flock or herd confers several advantages. The dominant animal has the first choice of food; if the source is spatially limited, as at a feeding table for birds, it may eat first, while the others follow in the order of their rank. In times of scarcity, social standing may determine survival; the lowest-ranking individuals, pushed to the outskirts of the feeding flock, careful to avoid the pecks or nips of their superiors as well as watching out for predators, may not manage to eat enough to keep alive. Low social rank appears to be one of the reasons why the juveniles of certain birds, such as Wood Pigeons in England, suffer much higher winter mortality than their elders. Dominant birds can occupy the most coveted places in a communal roost; and among polygamous animals of all kinds, the high-ranking males most often win females.

On its own territory, a bird is usually dominant, no matter how low it may rank on neutral territory—a fact that led Edwin Willis (1967) to define territory as "a space in which one animal or group generally dominates others which become dominant elsewhere." The farther from their own territory they wander in search of food, the lower a number of jays, titmice, thrushes, and other birds fall in social rank, or perhaps it would be more correct to say that they become more timid and submissive. Animals of nearly every kind feel more confident on their own home ground.

Although not absent from free animals in their natural environment, peck orders and similar manifestations of social rank are most conspicuous in domestic animals, animals in confinement, animals at feeding stations, and in other more or less artificial situations. In such situations social hierarchies have been chiefly studied. Certainly the kind of despotism that has been observed among penned chickens is rare among wild birds, which are free to go elsewhere if too greatly harassed by their companions in the flock.

In many social animals in their natural state, the high-ranking individual is not the despot but the leader, the vigilant guardian, the group protector occupying the post of danger, the peacemaker when disputes arise, like the patriarch among gorillas, the matriarch among Red Deer, the senior male in a group of cooperatively breeding Jungle Babblers. The true leader does not push his followers away from food and water but sees that they have what they need. Alexander of Macedonia, for all his faults, showed his true greatness as a leader when, marching on foot over sandy wastes under a blazing sun at the head of his army, tormented by thirst like all his men and barely able to stagger onward, he was given a helmet full of water, all that his scouts could find. Since it was impossible to divide so little water among so great a multitude, after thanking the scouts, Alexander poured it on the ground in full view of his troops, thereby raising their spirits as much as if each had received a drink—one of the finest things Alexander ever did, remarked his biographer, Arrian.

Much has been made of peck orders and other manifestations of dominance hierarchies as a method of social integration. But animals do not associate with others of their kind in order to be pecked, nipped, butted, or otherwise mistreated and made to feel inferior. Perhaps, however, their need to keep close company with others—for protection, for help in finding food, or just for companionship—is so great that they are willing to endure such treatment rather than remain solitary. Peck orders and the like appear to be developments whereby animals that are imperfectly social manage to remain together without too much discord. If such animals must compete for precedence, vent their irritation with each other, and otherwise display unfriendly attitudes, it is better that they promptly decide who comes first, who has the power to domineer the others, and that they preserve this order, than that they bicker continually over food, sleeping places, and other benefits. In some animals, we notice great disparity between the need for social cooperation and adaptation to social life. In our own species, this disparity is tragic: we yearn to love and to be loved; yet so great are our asperities and imperfections of character that our attempts to cultivate intimate, enduring relations with others often end in bitterness.

Of all animals, the termites and social Hymenoptera seem most perfectly fitted for social life; yet the price of this adaptation appears to have been loss of individuality. In the most highly social birds that I have studied, not dominance but perfect amity and equality appeared to prevail. Let us now examine the true bonds that hold animal societies together.

THE SOCIAL BONDS

The life of many animals is a compromise between social and anti-social tendencies. Even when they associate in large companies, these imperfectly social animals hold one another more or less aloof, each surrounding itself with a space within which it does not will-ingly permit its companions to intrude. This "Individual distance," as it has been called, is a sort of mobile territory with invisible boundaries that envelops the animal wherever it goes. P. J. Conder (1949) noticed that resting Black-headed Gulls maintain an indi-vidual distance of about one body-length; but when searching for food, their separation becomes greater. Tufted Ducks on a lake in St. James's Park in London stayed two or three body-lengths apart. Swallows resting on a wire seldom perch in contact but are often strung out at short and rather even intervals. Frequently the indi-vidual distance is the reach of a perching bird's bill.

The most social birds, however, show no such coolness toward their companions. While studying Groove-billed Anis, I noticed no antagonism between the members of a group, no attempt of one to dominate another. These highly social, communal-nesting, black cuckoos widespread in tropical America rest during the day, and roost at night, perching in a row and pressing as close together as they can. If a bird in the middle flies away, the remaining ones promptly sidle together and close the gap. Several species of wood-swallows studied by K. Immelmann (1966) in Australia perched in equally compact rows. In Kenya, V. G. L. van Someren (1956) found from two to six White-cheeked Colies, known also as mouse-birds, clinging upright to a leafy branch, abdomen pressed against abdomen. Among other birds that bunch together in groups con-

Blue-tailed Bee-eaters, *Merops superciliosus*

taining more than a single pair, at least when roosting at night, are Splendid Blue Wrens, Blue-tailed Bee-eaters, Long-tailed Titmice, and hanging parakeets. Cold weather often induces clustering by birds that ordinarily avoid contact with each other.

Among the bonds that hold social animals together, not the least important is reciprocal preening or grooming. Probably the majority of birds preen only themselves. Others, including pigeons, parrots, toucans, and many more preen their mates, especially about the head and neck, where the feathers are inaccessible to a bird's own bill. But in the most sociable of all, members of a flock appear to preen one another indiscriminately. When anis perch in a row, any one may nibble the feathers of any other. In the days when the valley where I live was still wild, Marbled Wood-Quails, now so rare and shy that they are seldom seen, were so tame that I could sometimes watch them for long intervals while standing unconcealed only a few yards away. They were especially easy to observe when they foraged at the woodland's edge. After scratching for food among fallen leaves, to the accompaniment of soft, melodious, contented notes, a covey of six began to put their feathers in order. Three rested close together on a low branch, alternately billing one another's plumage, chiefly on the head and abdomen. The one in the center performed this service for its companions on either side, who reciprocated the favor; and sometimes an outside bird reached past the central one to bill the plumage or legs of the quail on the other end. Presently a fourth bird jumped up to join the preening party on the branch, while the remaining two were similarly engaged on the ground. None tried to dominate another (Skutch 1983).

Among primates, mutual grooming is a prominent activity that probably helps to counteract the disruptive aggressiveness of some species, particularly baboons. So important is mutual grooming to male lemurs that their dentition has been highly modified to facilitate this activity: the front teeth of the lower jaw project forward as a sort of comb, which appears so poorly fitted for biting or chewing that it puzzled naturalists until they discovered that it serves excellently for grooming (Jolly 1967). The true monkeys and apes work over one another's pelage with their fingers rather than their teeth, removing dirt and external parasites. This widespread primate habit persists among humans with inadequate facilities for washing. In the highlands of Guatemala, where cold air and rarity of large streams discourage bathing, I used to see Indian women sitting in the doorways of their huts, diligently searching their children's hair for lice or whatever infested it. Horses, although imperfectly social, nibble each other simultaneously, mostly on the withers at the posterior end of the mane. My stallion and mare regularly exchanged this courtesy after their evening meal; yet, far from being a perfect gentleman, he would drive her from her bananas if he finished before she did.

Not only does help in body maintenance bind social animals more closely together; it may even draw animals of diverse kinds together. A number of birds regularly pluck parasites from the bodies of large mammals. In Africa, two species of sharp-toed oxpeckers, belonging to the starling family, persistently climb over the bodies of rhinoceroses, zebras, domestic cattle, and other herbivores, relieving them of the ticks and other pests that supply most of these birds' food. In the Americas, cowbirds of several species perform the same service for cattle and for free animals such as Capybaras and tapirs. Similarly, the Egyptian Plover plucks parasites from the thick hides of crocodiles and even, if Herodotus and Pliny were well informed, enter their huge mouths to clean between their teeth. Although all these great animals are amazingly tolerant of their feathered attendants, none seems to go out of its way to secure their services (Howell 1979).

The situation among certain fish is quite different. According to a review by W. Wickler (1968), the warmer waters of the oceans contain no less than forty-two species of fish belonging to fourteen families known as "cleaners." These fish specialize in plucking from the bodies of other fish of different kinds the bacteria and external parasites that adhere to them, as well as removing loose or dead skin and particles of food. The clients, often very much larger than their attendants, even open their mouths and raise their gill covers to permit the cleaners to enter and search through the gills. The cleaners profit by eating what they remove from their clients, while the latter are benefited by this cleansing of their bodies, so that this is an excellent example of mutually beneficial symbiosis. The client fish make a practice of visiting the coral reefs where the cleaners dwell, for a periodic grooming. The latter fearlessly approach fish that could easily swallow them and gently work over their bodies, removing foreign matter. Occasionally, perhaps in consequence of a misunderstanding, a cleaner is devoured by its client.

As too often happens when a pleasant community of interests grows up in the natural world or among people strangers butt in to take a base advantage of the situation. One of the cleaner fish *Labroides dimidiatus,* is mimicked by a quite different fish, *Aspidontus taeniatus,* of the same size and similarly marked with wide, longitudinal black bands on a light ground. Advancing under false colors, the sharp-toothed *Aspidontus,* instead of grooming the client, bites pieces from its caudal fin. Despite the close resemblance of the imitator to the cleaner in appearance and mannerisms, the clients learn to distinguish them; young, inexperienced individuals appear to be the chief victims of the deception.

Another social bond is cooperation in feeding. Probably most flocking birds, from pelicans diving for fish in the ocean to swifts catching flying insects high in the air, help one another to find the richest concentrations of their appropriate food. Oceanic birds, which are often dazzling white, or black and white, can see each other from afar and, when they notice a few of their kind repeatedly plunging upon a school of small fish or a concentration of squid, hasten to join the feast. Similarly, swifts coursing over a wide area can watch each other flying above the treetops and converge on the spot where continued circling reveals the presence of many small volitant creatures. Much closer cooperation in foraging was exhibited by the Marbled Wood-Quails already mentioned. Standing almost above them, I noticed not the slightest resentment when one picked food from a space that another had just cleared by scratching, sometimes removing it almost from beneath the scratcher's body. If one found something too large to swallow all at once, it did not run away with its prize, as domestic chickens do, but amicably permitted its companions to share the item. Yet all these quails appeared equally mature and able to forage for themselves.

Many birds wander through the woodland in mixed flocks, which are especially large and diverse in tropical forests. The members of such flocks have different foraging habits: some climb over the trunks of trees, plucking insects and spiders from crevices in the bark; others ransack dead leaves lodged in crotches and tangles of vines; others glean caterpillars and spiders from living foliage; still others dart into the air for flying insects. Although the birds in these motley flocks are predominantly insectivorous rather than frugivorous, and so take much the same food, the help that they incidentally give one another seems to outweigh competition. The insect put to flight by a bark-searcher or a leaf-gleaner is snatched up by a vigilant flycatcher. The continuous movements and varied calls of the birds in these parties make them so conspicuous that raptors should have no difficulty finding them; but the advantage of having many sharp eyes to detect an approaching enemy out-weighs the hazard of conspicuousness, so that the birds are safer in the motley flocks than they would be alone. Besides greater ease in finding food, probably a feeling of greater security induces these birds to forage in the mixed associations.

By placing food in each other's mouths, animals establish a still closer bond. Birds of many kinds feed their mates, most frequently as the breeding season approaches and while incubation is in progress. Usually the male gives food to the female; but occasion-ally she passes a morsel to him, as I have seen in the White-flanked Antwren and the Tawny-bellied Euphonia and L. de K. Lawrence (1968) saw in the Evening Grosbeak. By repeatedly feeding the male Andean Hillstar that has entered her territory in the high Peruvian Andes to court her, the female overcomes his timidity in a strange situation, without known parallel in the hummingbird family (Dorst 1962). More rarely, birds feed companions other than their mates: a group of Cedar Waxwings may pass a berry back and forth until finally one swallows or drops it. Scattered through the literature are instances of impaired adult birds remain-ing alive and in fair condition, apparently supplied by their com-panions with all the food they needed: a blind American White Pelican, a blind Indian Crow, a Brown Booby with only one wing, a Magnificent Frigatebird in similar plight, a Fiery-billed Aracari with a badly deformed beak, an ailing Gray Wood-Swallow, and a wounded Fijian White-breasted Wood-Swallow. It is not evident that all these crippled or sick birds were actually seen to receive food from others; but in British Columbia N. A. M. Verbeek and R. W. Butler (1981) repeatedly saw a male Northwestern Crow feed a female—not his mate—who had a blind eye and a deformed bill.

The importance of food as a social bond reaches its climax among the most highly social of all animals, the termites and the social Hymenoptera. W. M. Wheeler (1928) applied the name "trophallaxis" to the continual exchange of food, or at least of gustatory satisfactions, which he regarded as the most compelling attraction between all the members of an insect community. Termites are constantly feeding each other, with nourishment extruded either from the mouth or from the opposite end of the body, a practice that led Maeterlinck (1927) to characterize a termitary as a "collective coprophagy." By these exchanges, they infect each other with the intestinal protozoa without which many species of termites cannot assimilate their ligneous meals. In certain termites, the queen of a colony, whose huge swollen abdomen has become a factory for turning out endless eggs, exudes from her skin a substance so highly relished by the workers who feed her that sometimes, in their eagerness for more, they tear little strips from her cuticle to reach the underlying source. Small brown scars mark the spots where she has been wounded by her progeny.

The larvae of certain ants and wasps secrete from their salivary glands, or from relatively enormous glandular growths surrounding the mouth, substances that their nurses greedily lick up after feeding them. Naturally, the quantity of nourishment given by the attendants to the larvae far exceeds what they receive from them; otherwise, the young insects could not grow. But the larval secretions are so highly attractive that the workers will relinquish much food to obtain them; as a farmer will sometimes sell pounds of his produce in order to buy a few ounces of some delicacy. Adult ants of the same colony habitually feed each other with nutriment regurgitated from their "social stomachs." Wheeler held that neither affection nor cleanliness is the motive for the mutual licking in which ants indulge; they do so to enjoy the fatty exudates and other secretions of each other's bodies. If Wheeler's interpretation is correct, gustatory and olfactory pleasure—or, more technically, the stimulation of their chemoreceptors—is the reward for which the workers among the social insects lead their strenuous lives, cooperate closely with one another, and faithfully attend the helpless members of their community, including the egg-producing females, the larvae, and sometimes also the males. And who would begrudge them such small delights?

Among the attractions that bring animals together, we must not overlook the communal roost, which as night approaches draws to a central point, often in tremendous numbers, birds that during the day have been widely scattered in smaller groups or singly. The roosts of such birds as starlings, pigeons, swallows, crows, and others are too well known to need description here. Often birds of a number of species sleep close together in a clump of tall bamboos or a high stand of grass or reeds. In inclement weather, many individuals of a species that is usually less gregarious may crowd into a cavity that offers some protection. In the western United States, O. A. Knorr (1957) found as many as a hundred and fifty Pygmy Nuthatches lodging in an old pine trunk that contained several holes, at least one hundred of them in the same cavity. In the Costa Rican mountains, during the season of chilling rainstorms, I once, to my great delight, watched sixteen Prong-billed Barbets enter a hole in a tree so small that they must have slept in layers. Yet, when nesting, these barbets are highly territorial (Skutch 1989).

Finally, we cannot lightly dismiss the desire for companionship, divorced from any purely utilitarian motive, as a factor that draws individuals together, at least among the higher animals. Deprived of companions of their own species, animals sometimes become closely attached to an individual of some very different species. W. H. Hudson told of a lone swan that sought the company of a horse. Such incongruous partnerships as that of a dog and a deer, a cat and a rabbit, or a crow and an owl, have been so frequently recorded in the annals of natural history that it seems superfluous to elaborate the point.

It will be noticed that in the foregoing discussion of the social bonds nothing was said about sex. The omission is deliberate. Sex itself is not a cohesive but a disruptive factor in animal life. As already noted, gregarious mammals and birds, which through the long annual interval of sexual quiescence have lived together amicably, become mutually antagonistic as their reproductive urges awaken; coursing through their veins like some subtle venom, the sexual hormones make implacable enemies of erstwhile companions. Sex, in itself, forges no lasting bonds even between individuals of opposite sexes. Unless sexual partners are held together by some shared occupation or interest, such as caring for their offspring, or by personal liking or attachment not dependent upon primary sexual activity, male and female separate and go their own ways after the exhaustion of their erotic ardor. This applies to humans no less than to the rest of the animal kingdom, the chief exceptions being species in which a degenerate male lives permanently attached to the female in parasitic dependence, as in angler fish. Failure to recognize these truths has led certain anthropologists to attribute to the absence of an annual interval of sexual quiescence in humans a role in human social development that does not belong to it. Only indirectly, as the necessary prelude to the generation of offspring whose care unites the two parents in a shared activity, has sex contributed importantly to sociality in people and other animals.

Cooperation in Nesting and Attending Young

Sea birds of many kinds may be constrained to nest colonially by the paucity of islets or forbidding cliffs where alone they find adequate protection for their eggs and young. The massing of nests of gulls, terns, gannets, boobies, penguins, and other marine birds does not necessarily imply cooperation among them, although sometimes, as among murres, or guillemots, they minister to their neighbors' young.

Colonial nesting has a different aspect when several or many nests are contained in a single massive structure built by the occupants themselves. Among the conspicuous features of Hispaniola are the nests of Palm-Chats, distant relatives of waxwings, nearly always situated in the crown of one of the stately Royal Palms so abundant on that large Caribbean island. One such nest was a mass of interlaced twigs that I estimated to be ten feet high by four in diameter (3 by 1.2 meters). At a much smaller nest, I counted about twenty-five of the starling-sized brown birds with streaked white breasts flying back and forth, bringing more sticks. These great nests are avian apartment houses, containing many chambers that do not connect internally. Each chamber appears to be occupied by a single breeding pair; the birds domestic activities remain to be thoroughly studied. The same palm that upholds the Palm-Chats' massive structure may contain in its columnar trunk numerous holes of the Hispaniolan Woodpecker, one of the few members of this great family that nests colonially. In one trunk with twenty-four holes, I found four pairs of woodpeckers nesting simultaneously, and others seemed to be preparing to do so.

Nests of similar size are made by the Monk Parakeet, or Cotorra, of Argentina, one of the few parrots that builds instead of nesting in a cavity in tree or cliff. Strongly constructed of interlaced thorny twigs, the nests may hang from outer branches of trees or even from a large palm frond. They may attain a height of seven feet (2.1 meters), weigh a quarter of a ton, and provide separate, unconnected chambers for up to a dozen pairs of the parakeets, each of which lays four to eight dull white eggs in an unlined compartment that is approached through a porch or vestibule from a downwardly directed entrance (Conway 1965).

Of quite different construction, and even more ponderous, are the apartment houses of the Sociable Weaver. In one of the scattered trees in arid Namibia (formerly Southwest Africa), Herbert Friedmann (1930) found an edifice that measured about twenty-five by fifteen feet at the base by five in height (7.6 by 4.6 by 1.5 meters). To start such a construction, the whole flock of sparrow-sized birds, working together, builds a spreading roof by interlacing coarse dry grasses and small twigs. Beneath this general covering each pair attaches its own nest made of similar materials, until the lower surface of the mass is perforated by small, circular openings—nearly a hundred in the very large structure found by Friedmann. Each year the birds attach new nests below the old ones, until finally the overladen branch breaks beneath the weight of the huge edifice. Like the Palm-Chats and the Monk Parakeets, the weaver birds sleep in their nests even when they are not breeding, thereby saving much energy on chilly desert nights and decreasing their need of food.

Sociable Weavers, *Philetairus socius*,
at their many-chambered nest

Still closer cooperation in breeding is practiced by the lanky black anis we have already had occasion to mention. Although a pair will often nest alone, frequently two, three, or even more pairs join forces to build a simple, open nest of coarse sticks, which they line with green leaves that are brought daily until the young hatch. In this broad, open bowl the females lay their chalky white eggs in a common heap. All the participating anis of both sexes take turns incubating, one at a time, and later all feed the nestlings, making no distinction between their own offspring and those of their coworkers. Each night a single male takes charge of the eggs or nestlings. Bold in the defense of their families, Groove-billed Anis have often buffeted the back of my head while I looked into their nest (Skutch 1983).

Although Palm-Chats, Monk Parakeets, and Sociable Weavers build compound nests in which each pair occupies a separate chamber, and anis make a simple nest in which several pairs raise a compound family, another mode of cooperation is much more widespread among birds: a single breeding pair is assisted by one or more nonbreeding helpers. At the bulky nests of sticks built by the big, raucous Brown Jays in Caribbean Central America, the mated pair is usually aided by younger birds that are readily distinguished by their bills, colored black and yellow in the most diverse patterns. Once I watched seven grown jays, including the parents and five helpers, feed and guard a brood of three nestlings; every nest that I studied had at least one young assistant. These helpers sometimes fed the incubating female. In a population of Florida Scrub Jays, Glen E. Woolfenden (1975) learned that nearly all the yearlings helped their parents to feed and defend nestlings and fledglings, and about half the two-year-old jays did so. Breeding pairs assisted by their older, nonbreeding offspring produced substantially more young than did pairs without helpers.

Beneath heavy rain forest in the Caribbean lowlands of Costa Rica, long burrows in the ground, which in one case sheltered a brood of three nestlings, were attended by three or four White-fronted Nunbirds, all bringing food in their vivid orange-red bills. In England, a cozy nest of Long-tailed Tits is often attended by one or two adults in addition to the parents, all bringing food in perfect harmony. In the highlands of Guatemala, the beautiful, lichen encrusted, downy pouches of Bush-Tits attract from one to three unmated birds wearing the black facial masks of the males. These helpers sometimes brood as well as feed the four nestlings. As a reward for their services, they are permitted to sleep with the parents and young in the swinging pouch, during the cold nights of high altitudes.

In Australia, breeding pairs of Superb Blue Wrens are often assisted by extra males, usually their offspring of earlier years. Ian Rowley's (1965) careful studies showed that pairs with helpers raised nearly twice as many nestlings per nest as unassisted pairs, and about 50 percent more nestlings for each attendant adult. In many other resident birds of warmer regions, similar breeding groups, consisting of a mated pair with one or several unmated helpers, have been discovered; and the list of avian species that practice such cooperation continues to grow as tropical birds are more extensively studied (Brown 1987, Skutch 1987, Stacey and Koenig 1990).

Among the many modes of mutual aid among birds, none is more surprising than that practiced by the unhatched chicks of certain nidifugous species. The slight sounds made by quail chicks, as they break out of the eggshell, stimulate somewhat younger chicks in other eggs in the same nest to pip their shells sooner than they would otherwise do, with the result that all hatch more or less simultaneously and can be more promptly led off to the feeding ground by their parents. This doubtless unconscious cooperation contrasts strongly with the behavior of the young of certain raptorial birds, which—sometimes when only a few days old—murder, and perhaps afterward devour, their slightly younger or weaker nest mates, thereby removing competition for food (Johnson 1969).

Sometimes a lactating female mammal will suckle an orphaned young, of her own or even another species; as when a Blue Wildebeest who had lost her calf gave milk to a motherless Burchell's Zebra. But helpers do not fit into the mammalian system of reproduction as readily as they do into the avian system and, with the

exception of a few cases reported for jackals and wolves, cooperation in rearing the young is largely limited to protecting the mother
and her offspring. Among elephants, zebras, wild horses, and horned
quadrupeds of various kinds, the males defend the females and
young. When threatened by wolves or other predators, Muskoxen
of the Arctic tundra form a circle around the calves, presenting
their horns in unbroken array against the enemy. The Malayan
Gaur, or Seladang, a wild relative of domestic cattle, travels through
jungle and neighboring clearings in herds of a dozen or more individuals, led by a large, wary cow. From a crow's nest high in a tree-
top, L. Weigum (1970) enjoyed the rare experience of watching
such a herd when a marauding tiger approached. Hearing the
carnivore's rumbling, the old cows advanced toward it, while the
master bull guarded the calves. After the cows had located the
marauder, the bull, bellowing and snorting, rushed toward it with
lowered horns and put it to flight.

On the African savannas, baboons travel in large companies,
with the females and infants surrounded by the adult males. About
twice the size of the females, the males have much bigger canine
teeth, useful for defending the troop from leopards and other enemies. Policemen of the society, the dominant males stop fights
among their subordinates, often simply by means of a masterful
stare. Monkeys also travel in troops, in which childless females
eagerly fondle infants not their own. Occasionally, even a male will
carry an orphaned baby, as C. R. Carpenter (1934) noticed in the
Howling Monkey of tropical America. Living in trees through which
they can flee more rapidly than can pursuing mammals, monkeys
are less exposed to danger than are the largely terrestrial baboons,
and their troops are less tightly organized.

The foregoing examples of cooperation in the living world are
only a small selection from the vast body of similar facts that naturalists have gathered, chiefly in the present century; but they amply
confirm what Kropotkin tried to prove with the more meager data
available when he wrote, that mutual aid is widespread among animals and has powerfully influenced their evolution. Harmonization
is active not only within organisms, in their growth and functioning,

but likewise between them, joining members of a species in cooperative societies and even bringing diverse species together in mutually beneficial associations. This harmonization or pacification of the living world has still not progressed very far; the cooperating groups exist precariously in the midst of strife, and even within them concord is often far from perfect. Yet cooperation no less than competition is widespread in nature, and must receive serious consideration by any evolutionary philosophy.

5

Exploitation and Cooperation

As we have seen, the living world is full of inconsistencies, or situations that one would not expect to follow from their antecedents. Among its many paradoxes is that organisms which, to the best of their ability, insulate themselves from everything around them nevertheless need surrounding things to support their lives; whereas lifeless objects, which do not separate themselves by special coverings from other things but mingle freely with them, have in general no need of insulation. Rocks, many metals, and the more stable crystals might continue indefinitely to exist in a vacuum; living organisms need constant support by their environment, and most of them are, in one way or another, dependent upon other organisms.

Dependence has degrees. Green plants, able to elaborate their own food by photosynthesis, are far more independent than animals. Their basic needs are sunlight, air, water, and elements dissolved in water or in the soil. Probably most of them could thrive as isolated individuals, as many do scattered through arid deserts, in rock crevices at the highest altitudes where vegetation grows, and in scattered spots almost everywhere. Even those that thrive amid others, like trees in a forest or grasses in a close stand, may grow in isolation, sometimes better when less closely crowded by competitors for sunlight and water. However, many plants are less independent of other organisms than they appear. The tree that stands so proudly all alone may need the mycorrhizal fungi that

envelop its finer roots to absorb the water and solutes that it requires
from the soil. Plants that are not self-fertile need pollen from others
to set seeds. All whose pollen is not carried by wind or water are
dependent upon animals—insects, birds, bats, and others—to bring
it to them, and many employ animals to disperse their seeds. In the
living world as a whole, the most widespread mode of dependence
of one organism upon another is for reproduction. Even those that
as individuals can live quite alone would cease to exist as species
without other individuals to fecundate their reproductive cells.

Unable to synthesize their own food from inorganic materials,
all animals are strictly dependent upon plants, either directly or
indirectly, as when they eat other animals that are themselves nourished, often also indirectly, by vegetation. The dependence of one
organism upon another may be unilateral or reciprocal, exploitative or cooperative, in both relationships often complicated by
competition for resources. The effects of these two modes of interaction upon the creatures involved in them are among the greatest
contrasts that the living world presents.

Interactions among organisms fall into the following broad
categories:

> Exploitation of plants by plants
> Exploitation of animals by plants
> Exploitation of plants by animals
> Exploitation of animals by animals
> Cooperation among plants
> Cooperation between plants and animals
> Cooperation among animals

Let us briefly survey these relationships in this order.

EXPLOITATION OF PLANTS BY PLANTS

In the vegetable kingdom probably the most frequent, and certainly the most conspicuous, mode of unilateral exploitation is that
practiced by vines of all sorts, from slender twiners like morning

glories to massive lianas of tropical forests, all of which, having lost the capacity to hold themselves erect, grasp other plants to raise themselves into the sunshine. Usually they reduce the amount of light that falls upon the supporting plants, decreasing their photosynthesis. The more aggressive of them spread a smothering blanket of foliage over the crowns of the highest trees of the forest. Their constricting coils may strangle the tree up which they spiral; but sometimes the trunk grows over them and embeds them in its wood.

In abandoned clearings in humid forests, a riotous growth of vines and creepers burdens young trees, weighing them down or breaking their branches or trunks, making it difficult for them to rise above the welter, and delaying for years the reestablishment of the forest. Certain trees that frequently start life in such clearings have developed special strategies to meet this situation: the young trunk bears no branches, but only big leaves that perform their photosynthetic task and fall, giving the creepers no permanent hold, until the slender tree rises above encumbering vegetation and forms a spreading crown, in the manner of cecropia and jacaranda trees in tropical America. Many vines flower beautifully on the roof of the forest or nearer the ground, often at the expense of the host's own bloom.

Instead of climbing from the ground up to the light, epiphytes germinate and grow on trunks and branches, above all in the humid tropics. They depend upon the host only for support, while they make their own food in green leaves and derive their minerals from decaying bark and the vegetable debris that lodges among them. Some epiphytes send long roots to the ground, whence they draw water and minerals, while others catch and store rainwater in specially modified organs. In size, epiphytes range from trees that perch on other trees through a vast array of ferns, aroids, bromeliads, and orchids large and small to tiny mosses and liverworts. A moderate load of epiphytes appears to have no ill effects upon the plant that supports them but, especially in cloud forests on tropical mountains, the burden of these air plants may become so heavy that it breaks large boughs. With a wonderful diversity of colorful flowers and floral bracts, bromeliads, orchids, and other epiphytes adorn the trees on which they perch, usually below the high canopy, in the shade where bloom is scarce.

Most aggressive of all are the strangling fig trees, which from seeds deposited by fig-eating birds and other animals on high limbs start life as epiphytes but send roots to the ground along the trunk of the host tree. As they thicken, these roots meet and coalesce, until the supporting trunk is enveloped by a massive network. After the strangled trunk dies and decays, the fig tree remains standing on a high cylinder of fused roots, through the gaps in which one can look. Some of these usurping figs are among the giants of tropical forests.

The exploitation of plants by plants reaches a more advanced stage in the half-parasites or water-parasites, which might be described as green epiphytes that synthesize their own food but draw water and minerals from the host plant's vessels by means of haustoria that penetrate its tissues. Best-known and most abundant of the water-parasites are the mistletoes of the family Loranthaceae, with about one thousand three hundred species distributed over most of Earth, chiefly in the tropics and subtropics. A few make colorful floral displays on high boughs, but a heavy infestation may kill the supporting tree. Their fruits are eaten by many birds and are a principal food of several species of both the Old World and the New. After digesting off the pulp, the birds void the seeds surrounded by mucilage that attaches them to branches on which they happen to fall, where they germinate and grow.

Among flowering plants, full parasites are rare. Some are inconspicuous plants of humid forests, where they grow upon roots of other plants in the dark undergrowth. Their leaves, reduced to scales, are devoid of chlorophyll, making them wholly dependent upon their hosts, or associated fungi, for nourishment. The parasite may be white, yellowish, purplish, brownish, or dark red. Their flowers may be small and inconspicuous or very big, like the yard-broad flower of *Rafflesia arnoldii* of Sumatra, reputed to be the largest in the world. Much more numerous than fully parasitic flowering plants are parasitic fungi, which attack agricultural plants of many

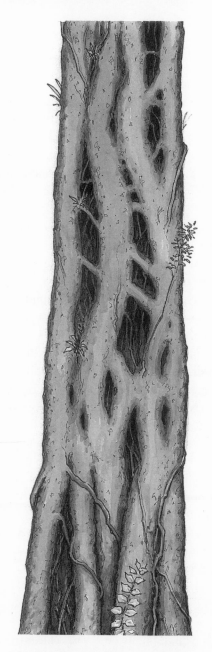

Aerial roots of an epiphytic fig tree
strangling trunk of the host tree

kinds as well as forest trees, often causing heavy losses if not com-
bated with fungicides that help to pollute the environment. Parasitic
fungi are apparently derived from saprophytic forms that play an
indispensable role in nature's economy by decomposing dead vegetation of all kinds, returning its mineral contents to the soil, where
the minerals are picked up by the roots of living plants. Without
these saprophytes, woodlands would become impenetrable mazes
of fallen trunks and branches because termites and other insects
would hardly suffice to reduce to humus all the debris of thriving
forests.

A wide survey of exploitation in the vegetable kingdom reveals
that it is caused chiefly by severe competition for living space and
sunlight. Many plants, the vines and epiphytes, solve their problem
by climbing over other plants or perching upon them. Those that
grow upon others, often far above the ground, sometimes find it
expedient to draw sap from their hosts; instead of sending roots
down to the soil, they become half-parasites. A different set of plants,
mostly growing in deep shade, have become full parasites, often on
the roots of their hosts. None of these dependent plants has anything to gain by killing its host; the liana or epiphyte falls with the
tree that supports it; the half-parasite or full parasite dies with the
plant on which it grows. Aside from parasitic fungi, the chief vegetable enemies of trees are the lianas that weigh them down, smother
them, or constrict their trunks. In contrast to the situation among
animals, exploitation of plants by plants has no psychic effects
upon them, or none detectable by us. It is so slow and silent that it
hardly distresses the most sensitive onlooker. By greatly diversify-
ing vegetable forms, it has made the vegetable world more interesting, and given us the beauty of orchids, most of the more spectacular of which grow as epiphytes.

EXPLOITATION OF ANIMALS BY PLANTS

Animals, which exploit plants on a vast scale, are rarely exploited
by them. The carnivorous flowering plants, which by traps and pit-
falls the most diverse capture and digest insects and other small

invertebrates, and occasionally a diminutive vertebrate, are a very minor element of the flora that deserves a separate chapter. A family of fungi, the Entomophthoraceae, contains numerous species that infest the tissues of flies, caterpillars, and other small creatures, killing and devouring them. Other fungi exploit larger animals, including humans, causing irritating skin infections and more serious diseases.

EXPLOITATION OF PLANTS BY ANIMALS

The only animals that do not exploit plants directly are the carnivores or insectivores that do so indirectly, by devouring creatures directly nourished by plants; or sometimes, in long food chains, nutrients obtained directly from plants pass through diverse animal bodies before they reach the ultimate predator. Recent investigations of the upper levels of tropical rain forests suggest that the number of insect species may run into millions, and a large proportion of them devour the tissues of living plants. Most conspicuous is their damage to foliage; if they do not defoliate a whole tree, they may leave few intact leaves upon it. Swarms of locusts may devastate a wide area. Less noticeable but almost equally damaging to plants are the depredations of a host of small, seed-eating beetles that may ruin the seed crop of a tree. The relation of butterflies to plants is ambivalent: caterpillars devour much foliage; the winged adults into which they metamorphose make some amends by serving as pollinators, although often not of plants that nourished their larval stage, as would be just.

Vertebrate animals that exploit plants unilaterally include the grazers, the browsers, and the seed eaters. Horses and their kin are most at home on wide, open grasslands, over which they roam in small or large herds. Over the ages, typical grazers and their food plants have coevolved, not in a direct, one-species-to-one-species pattern but in a more diffuse manner; many of the grazers involved in this secular interaction have disappeared from Earth, and perhaps some of the grasses that nourished them have also become extinct. By the basal growth of their leaves, grasses are as well adapted to support grazing that is not excessive as, by dentition and digestive system, the grazers are to crop and digest them. By preventing the accumulation of dead blades that reduce photosynthesis and invite fires, moderate grazing appears to benefit well-adapted grasses.

Browsers gather foliage, often together with branches and flowers, above the ground. Probably the most highly specialized of extant browsers is the giraffe, whose long neck, with associated modifications of the vascular system, enable it to reach green shoots too high for all its four-footed competitors. Although primarily grazers, horses are often tempted to browse upon the foliage of shrubs or trees within their reach. Cows browse as readily as they graze, as do a number of kinds of antelope and deer. At higher levels, sloths and monkeys browse upon the foliage of a variety of trees and vines, which for some species, like howler monkeys, is a principal food. Fairly large birds, such as grouse in northern woodlands and guans in tropical American forests, browse freely on foliage and buds, often high in trees. Among reptiles, iguana lizards eat leaves. Grazing and browsing mammals serve the plants among which they move by dispersing seeds that cling to their hair by means of hooks or sticky secretions. Many of these animals vary their diet of green herbage when they find tasty fruits, with seeds that may pass unharmed through their alimentary canals and thus be widely spread. The fragrant fruits of guava trees are eagerly sought by horses, cattle, and other animals, which scatter the hard, indigestible little seeds through pastures and fields where many seedlings spring up.

Among the exploiters of plants are seed-eating birds and rodents. Although some members of the large parrot family are nectar drinkers and pollinators, the majority are seed predators, using thick, doubly hinged bills to extract nutritious embryos from seed coats that are often hard. With strong, crushing bills, grosbeaks and other finches remove embryos from hard-shelled seeds. Little goldfinches and many seed-eaters that swarm in tropical grasslands prefer smaller seeds that they can swallow whole. Cross-bills with overlapping mandibles pluck seeds from the scaly cones of pines and other coniferous trees. Squirrels, agoutis, rats, and other rodents devour many seeds. Seed predators—both invertebrate, like many beetles, and vertebrate, like a number of birds and mammals—greatly reduce the reproductive potential of the plants that supply them with rich sources of energy. However, certain jays and nutcrackers among birds, agoutis and squirrels among rodents, compensate the sources of their seeds by burying a few or many for future use. The forehanded animal may die or forget some of its hidden seeds, which upon germinating, perhaps at a distance from the parent tree or shrub, propagate the species.

Among grazers, browsers, and seedeaters are many highly gregarious mammals and birds, which through much of the year live in peace with others of their own and of different species. In general, they neither fear one another nor are feared by animals of different habits. Mutual aid in avoiding or repelling predators is frequent among them, as told in chapter 4. Conflicts arise among the males of these vegetarians mainly in the mating season, when they contend for females, often fiercely. Unless their populations become excessive, they do no great harm to the plants that support them: grasses are well able to withstand grazing; seeds of many plants are produced in such abundance that the existence of their species is not jeopardized by the consumption of many of their embryos; vigorous trees and shrubs can replace lost foliage.

More harmful to vegetation appear to be the largely terrestrial mammals and birds that dig up and devour the subterranean storage organs, rich in starch and other nutrients, of many herbaceous and suffrutescent plants—their tubers, corms, bulbs, and thickened roots. On the whole less gregarious than grazers, browsers, and seed predators, they tend to forage alone or in small groups, which is fortunate for the plants they eat. While humans were in the hunting and gathering stage, the storage organs that they extracted from the soil with digging sticks must have contributed substantially to their diets, but the extent of this injury to vegetation is now difficult to assess. Exceedingly harmful to plants are huge animals like elephants, which, where numerous, may destroy light woodlands by pushing over small trees to supply the immense quantity of provender that each individual needs every day.

The greatest, most destructive exploiter of vegetation, as of much else, is humankind. I refer not to agriculture, which is essentially a mode of cooperation between people and cultivated plants (although its side effects upon the native flora are often disastrous), but to the widespread destruction of trees to provide grazing for beef cattle, or to supply timber, pulpwood, charcoal, and other products. After destroying most broad-leaved forests in the North Temperate Zone of the Old World and the New, exploiters of trees and the lands on which they grow have been attacking tropical rain forests with such unrestrained greed that if this plundering cannot be halted, the forests will disappear in the next century. So great is this destruction that whole species of animals and plants are becoming extinct or have already vanished. The trees that people plant, as some slight compensation for the woods that we destroy, especially the all-too-common pines and eucalyptus, can never form forests of the magnificence and productivity, for creatures of many kinds, of those that we level.

EXPLOITATION OF ANIMALS BY ANIMALS

The exploitation of animals by animals has many aspects. Frequently the animals that are eaten are so different from their eaters that we do not think of this act as predation. Although the robin swallowing earthworms and the warbler catching insects are technically predators, we do not ordinarily place them in this category, to which we spontaneously assign the larger and fiercer carnivores—lions and wolves, eagles and falcons—that strike down, rend, and devour creatures of blood as red and warm as their own. The distinction we make between animals that devour creatures very different from themselves and those that prey upon animals in the same zoological class, or as highly evolved, as themselves has a valid foundation in the effects of their activities upon the animals themselves and upon the human onlooker. Although many people delight in the spectacle of violence and bloodshed of every sort (so long as they are not themselves hurt by it), the sensitive onlooker is shocked and distressed by the sight of a hawk seizing a piteously crying bird or a Cheetah tearing the vitals from a living antelope; but we are not so affected by a bird devouring a caterpillar. Our sympathy is not aroused by the insect or spider in the bill of a bird as it is by a songbird in the talons of a falcon or a mammal eviscerated by the fangs of another mammal.

As far as we can tell, predation by animals upon others much lower in the evolutionary scale does not have the same psychic effects upon either predator or prey as does predation upon birds and mammals. It is above all such predation that has burdened animals with their secondary nature and all the distressing attributes of the armature (chapter 3—ferocity, anger, hatred, fear, suspicion, callousness, and similar psychic states). Although predation by warm-blooded animals upon warm-blooded animals appears to be the chief cause of this lamentable development, carnivorous reptiles —snakes, crocodilians, monitor lizards—have contributed substantially to it. The human species, long a hunter of large animals and probably through long ages a frequent victim of the larger predatory mammals and reptiles, has been more heavily infected by these disturbing passions than has any other animal, possibly because our minds are more active and our emotions stronger. Only because we have hands to wield weapons have we managed to survive without protruding fangs, claws, horns, or similar organic growths, offensive or defensive, which the struggle between predator and prey has imposed upon creatures involved in it; and without a thick hide or protective carapace.

This rapid survey of the exploitation of animals by animals would be incomplete if we failed to mention the exploitation of females by males who fight among themselves for the females but contribute nothing to their offspring beyond a minuscule sperm. The psychic effects of such fighting and uncaring fatherhood are in some animals almost as unfortunate as those arising from predation. Even among men who in the present age mostly support and protect their children, an exploitative attitude toward the child-bearing sex persists in the guise of *machismo* or male chauvinism, which today is combatted by women seeking gender equality.

The exploitation of animals by a great variety of small parasites, internal and external, has been a major cause of suffering
and death, but its psychic effects have been very different from that
caused by large predators. We cannot fear or hate a protozoon or
fluke that we have never seen (and probably do not know about) as
we fear and hate a man-eating tiger or a shark. Fear of disease
tends to be more persistent but less paralyzingly intense than terror in the imminent presence of a huge ravening beast.

COOPERATION AMONG PLANTS

Turning now to the cooperative interactions of organisms, we find
that among plants they are chiefly passive. By growing close together,
plants may maintain an environment favorable to one another, as
among the trees of tropical rain forests. The mycorrhiza that
envelop the feeding roots of many of these trees, helping them to
absorb indispensable elements from the soil, are nourished by carbohydrates supplied by the trees in a mutually advantageous association. A similar symbiosis occurs between leguminous plants and
the bacteria that form nodules on their roots, absorbing free nitrogen from the air that permeates the soil and supplying their hosts
with nitrates in return for carbohydrates.

COOPERATION BETWEEN PLANTS AND ANIMALS

Plants, which for long ages have suffered uncomplainingly from
the depredations of animals, respond magnificently when animals
cooperate with them. The flowers that brighten woods and mead-
ows, adorn our festive occasions, express our sympathy with the
sick and the bereaved, and provide the motifs for so many paint-
ings and household decorations are displayed by plants to advertise
the availability of nectar to the bees, butterflies, other insects, birds,
and other creatures that convey pollen from the anthers of one to
the stigmas of another. Fragrance makes flowers more attractive to
insects as well as to the people who delight in them. Sweet nectar is
sometimes enriched with vitamins and amino acids; while pollen,

produced in excess of the plant's needs for fertilization, offers a nutritious food for the many kinds of bees that busily collect it in special baskets on their hindlegs, then carry it back to their hives and mix it with nectar to make "beebread."

Wind pollination is a wasteful but adequate method for plants that grow in almost pure stands, as in grasslands and northern woods. In rich tropical forests where trees of one kind tend to grow scattered among many other kinds, only insects or birds that, at least temporarily, confine their visits to a single species can efficiently pollinate them. We owe such forests to cooperation between animals and plants. We, who enjoy the colors and fragrance of flowers, the beauty, interest, and diverse products of tropical woodlands, are incidental beneficiaries of a mode of cooperation between animals and plants highly advantageous to both of them.

Although by hooks or other means of attaching inedible fruits to fur or clothing many plants exploit animals unilaterally to disperse their seeds, a great number of them reward the dispersers with food. Frugivorous birds—in contrast to seed predators like parrots—are by virtue of their numbers and mobility the chief disseminators of seeds, especially in tropical woodlands where dispersal by wind plays a subordinate role. After swallowing a many-seeded berry or a small, one-seeded drupe like a cherry, a bird rapidly digests the soft pulp. Small frugivores like tropical American euphonias and manakins may void the seeds in their droppings ten minutes or less after swallowing the fruit; larger species, like Eurasian Blackbirds, within half an hour. If, instead of passing the seeds through the length of the alimentary canal, the bird regurgitates them from its crop, it eliminates them much more rapidly. Such brief residence inside the bird does not injure seeds adapted for avian dispersal, which germinate where they fall, often at a distance from the plant that bears them (Snow and Snow 1988). We owe the colors, aroma, and nutritive value of a great diversity of fruits to a tacit compact between fructiferous plants and frugivorous birds. By selection, people have increased the size and flavor of fruits originally adapted for dispersal by birds, among which we might include cherries, currants, and strawberries. The wild ancestors of certain larger fruits improved and esteemed by humans—avocados in the New World, mangos in the Old—were probably disseminated by mammals. Again, we have benefited greatly from a mutually beneficial arrangement between plants and animals.

No mode of cooperation between animals and plants has had more momentous consequences, not only for us but for the whole living world and the planet that supports it, than agriculture. It would be superfluous to expatiate here upon the advantages, economic and aesthetic, moral and intellectual, that we have derived from cultivating plants in fields, orchards, and gardens. If we measure the success of a species by the number of its individuals and the extent of their dispersion over Earth, cultivars that people have improved and carefully tended for many centuries include some of the most successful of all plants. The association has been highly advantageous to both parties. Even the camp followers of cultivation, the unwanted plants that we call weeds, have profited greatly and spread widely over the world. Regrettably, agriculture has expanded at the expense of vast areas of splendid forests and the creatures they sheltered. By supporting excessively dense human populations, it has created many problems that never troubled peoples who lived as hunters and gatherers on the bounty of wild nature. Plants have responded generously to the care that we have bestowed upon them. It seems to be our turn to show our appreciation of the advantages plants have given us by using them with greater wisdom and moderation, restricting agriculture to soils best suited for it, and showing more concern for all the vegetable and animal species that thrive on uncultivated land without our help but often with mutually beneficial associations of their own.

Cooperation among Animals

Our association with domesticated animals has been less unequivocally commendable than that with cultivated plants. As with plants, some domestic animals are much more numerous and widespread than they might have become in the wild state, and by this criterion they are highly successful species; but with animals that enjoy and suffer, the relationship has other aspects that hardly apply to plants, which are less highly organized. Plutarch, defender of animals, held that it is not wrong to domesticate them so that we may be kind to them. When an animal that is gently treated, well fed, and cured when sick or injured pays for all this laborious attention by working for a master, we might regard this as a fair and mutually beneficial arrangement. But the animals that bear our burdens or haul our vehicles—the horse, the ox, the camel—do not understand why they are compelled to work; for them it is forced labor. Moreover, the situation has all the perils inseparable from arbitrary power. Too often the poor beast is underfed, overworked, its sores neglected. Plants cannot be cudgeled or goaded to increase their yield, as beasts of burden too often are to make them pull or bear loads too heavy for them.

Animals raised for their flesh are cruelly slaughtered, often after being abominably treated during their short lives. Only exceptionally, or in an indulgent mood, can we regard the human association with domestic animals as mutually beneficial cooperation. At best, many generations of compulsion have distorted the animals' hereditary patterns of behavior; they have in most cases been selected for docility rather than intelligence; their spontaneous impulses are thwarted, with the result that people who know only domestic animals tend to underestimate their minds—an assessment that might be corrected by wider familiarity with free ones.

Many examples of cooperation among animals have been given in preceding chapters, especially chapter 4. The first step in the formation of a cooperative society is the association of a male and female in attending their young, which is much more common in birds than in mammals. In many birds the association is very close, the two partners sharing rather equally all the tasks of rearing and protecting their offspring. When the pair remain together throughout the year and their young stay with them after becoming self-supporting, sociality takes a long step forward. This is the origin of cooperative breeding, which in its advanced stages is the highest development of family life among nonhuman vertebrates, equaled only by the most harmonious human households.

A cooperating group may consist of from three to, rarely, thirty-five individuals, as in the Chestnut-bellied Starling of Nigeria (Wilkinson 1982). Group members are usually closely related, most commonly offspring of the breeding pair, but outsiders may join the family and help with its chores. The arrangement has advantages for all participants. The parental task of rearing a brood is lightened by the help other group members give in feeding nestlings and fledglings, protecting them, and, in species that sleep in dormitory nests or cavities, putting the youngsters to bed. Parents with helpers may live longer and raise more young than those without them. The nonbreeding helpers benefit by being permitted to reside in relative safety on the parental domain instead of being expelled to confront an unfamiliar and perilous world soon after they can support themselves, as many young birds are. While assisting the breeding pair to rear nestlings that are usually their younger siblings, the helpers gain experience that will be valuable to them when, at the age of about two or more years, they emigrate, mate, and rear families of their own—or, in some species, they may set up housekeeping on the group's territory, which then contains several breeding pairs that reciprocally help one another, while receiving more aid from the younger, nonbreeding members of the association.

All who have carefully watched cooperatively breeding birds have commented upon the amity that prevails among group members, the rarity of conflict among them. Moreover, boundary disputes with adjoining groups tend to be settled by vocal and visual displays instead of crude fighting—peace conferences that actually keep the peace! Although probably no animal can exist in this competitive world with no vestige of its secondary nature, in these cooperative birds the armature has been attenuated. Their pacific character might be a direct expression of a primary nature that was never heavily loaded with secondary attributes, or, since many of them are probably descended from ancestors that were less social and pacific, it might be a result of socialization, as is evident in the young of certain cooperative breeders that become more disciplined as they mature in the midst of their families.

Unhappily, the small cooperative groups in which humans long lived did not settle their differences with neighboring groups by singing and dancing on opposite sides of a territorial boundary but resorted to more violent measures. These people, like many of us today, were laden with such an incredible hodgepodge of primary, secondary, and tertiary attributes that we wonder how they kept their sanity. Nevertheless, developments within these clans had far-reaching consequences for the future of humankind. When our remote ancestors abandoned the trees to live on the ground, they had grasping hands evolved for climbing. As these ancestors became able to walk erect, their hands, no longer needed for locomotion, became the most versatile manipulatory organs in the animal king-dom. The uses to which hands could be put gave to intelligence a survival value beyond what it could attain among animals in which lack of such flexible executive organs severely limits the practical value of whatever bright ideas they might have. Brains grew larger and intelligence increased to make the best use of these facile hands.

Despite much theorizing, the origin of language from the inar-ticulate cries of animals remains obscure. But, however language began, we can hardly doubt that the need to communicate while planning and executing constructive undertakings that required many hands accelerated its growth. A developed language is inti-mately related to constructive cooperation by primates equipped with efficient hands. Animals that join in activities no more con-structive than running down and tearing prey, like wolves and hye-nas, do not need articulate speech and, accordingly, never devel-oped it.

The ability to speak and exchange ideas with others stimulates thought and speculation. For a long while, human notions about ourselves and nature were crude and confused. With the develop-ment of agriculture and a settled instead of a nomadic life, a small minority enjoyed leisure to put their minds in order and think more deeply. They began to grope toward wider horizons and, with growing wisdom, their sympathies expanded. The Stoics taught that all good people everywhere are friends; Christians proclaimed the brotherhood of mankind; oriental religions inculcated respect for all creatures. Whatever their religion or philosophy—or lack of either—generous, sensitive spirits reach out with love and grateful appreciation toward an inclusive whole. That an animal insulated in a flexible skin to safeguard the delicately balanced physiological processes supporting each individual's life should expand spiritually and intellectually so far beyond the enclosing integument is the most unpredictable development, the greatest paradox, in the whole paradoxical realm of life. But perhaps, if our insight were deeper, we might recognize that the expansive human spirit is a flowering of tendencies present in the materials of which we all are made, a partial fulfillment of the universal movement to give value to Being by ordering its contents in patterns of increasing amplitude, complexity, and coherence.

6

Paradoxical Plants

Plants are independent, self-supporting organisms; animals are dependent upon them; from this fundamental difference most other far-reaching differences between plants and animals may be traced. A typical vascular plant is rooted in the ground, from which it draws the water and salts that it needs to maintain its independent life. Anchored in one spot, it is unable to change its location and, accordingly, it lacks both locomotor organs and sensory organs to guide them. Without such organs, a brain and central nervous system to receive information through the senses and direct the organism's course would be superfluous. Its movements are limited to alterations in the arrangement of its parts, especially foliage, by growth or changes in the turgor of its tissues, which may be slow or swift. A typical flowering plant stands erect with its roots in the soil, spreading its leaves in the sunlight. Less often it creeps over the ground, preserving its independence if not its upright posture.

A minority of plants compromise their independence for certain economies or other advantages. Most numerous in this category, as noted, are the vines that save the expense of forming self-supporting stems and rise more swiftly into the sunshine by twining around or clinging to other plants. As we have likewise seen, some plants become half-parasites, drawing sap from their hosts but retaining their green leaves and capacity for photosynthesis, like mistletoes. A few flowering plants lose their chlorophyll and become full parasites. Most surprising of all are the insectivorous or, more correctly, carnivorous plants, which in traps of great diversity catch and digest a great variety of small insects and other creatures, including an occasional vertebrate such as a tiny tadpole or hatchling fish, thereby obtaining nitrogenous compounds, phosphates, and other salts rare or lacking in the swamps, sphagnum bogs, or poor soil where many of them grow. Worldwide, about 450 species of dicotyledonous flowering plants, belonging to fifteen genera in six families, have adopted the carnivorous habit. Since all these plants retain their chlorophyll and capacity to synthesize carbohydrates, none is as completely dependent upon other organisms for food as animals are; but by feeding like animals many of them increase their growth

PITCHER PLANTS OR PITFALL TRAPS

The traps are all modified leaves, or parts of leaves. They may be passive, waiting motionless for victims to enter them, or active, moving to seize their prey or to hold it more securely. Among the former are the pitfall traps, shaped like pitchers or trumpets. Of these the best-known family is the Sarraceniaceae, or pitcher plant family, with nine species confined to eastern North America, from Labrador to Florida and westward to Iowa and Kentucky, with most species in the southeast. The pitcher may stand more or less upright, bearing above its mouth an expanded projection or arching hood, sometimes miscalled a lid; it does not close the pitcher but may diminish the amount of rain that falls into it. Or it may lie recumbent on the ground, like *Sarracenia psittacina*, with a recurved, cowled end that directs the narrow mouth horizontally toward the base of the tube. The slender upright pitcher of *S. flava* is often three feet (90 cm.) high by two or three inches (5 or 7.5 cm.) wide. All these pitchers have a broad or narrow wing along the front. They tend to be brightly decorated, with white, red, purple, or yellowish spots or stripes on a generally green ground. These colors not only attract insects but, together with the large, inverted, purple or yellow flowers raised on long stalks above the rosette of pitchers, they have induced horticulturists to grow them in cool greenhouses, making many hybrids.

A feature common to all carnivorous plants is an abundance of glands of diverse forms and functions, some of which lure visitors with nectar or sweetish mucilage, while others secrete enzymes to digest victims or to absorb the products of their dissolution. Drawn by its colors to a pitcher of *Sarracenia purpurea*, the Side-saddle Flower or Huntsman's Cup, an insect finds nectar glands scattered over its outer surface among abundant hairs. If, creeping over the exterior, it reaches the pitcher's mouth, it enters an insidious pitfall in which four zones are distinguished. The first is the cordate, emarginate hood, where the hairs amid the nectar glands point strongly downward, directing the creature inward to the second zone, which is a narrow collar of velvety aspect, covered with fine, downwardly directed ridges and many more glands. Sliding still farther inward while it enjoys the nectar, the deluded insect reaches zone three, which covers half of the pitcher's interior with a smooth, glassy, gland-dotted surface that precipitates it into the fourth zone. This pit is surrounded by long, slender, downward-pointing, glassy hairs, which impede the victim's escape. Here are no more nectar glands to solace it while it drowns or otherwise succumbs. Absence of a cuticle over much of this zone facilitates absorption.

Species of *Sarracenia* differ in the amount of water their pitchers contain before they open or which is secreted into them after opening. The liquid in young, unopened pitchers appears always to be sterile, but that into which animals have fallen contains bacteria, as is to be expected. In *Sarracenia*, as in other carnivorous plants, the possibility of decomposition by bacterial action has persistently plagued the interpretation of the many experiments designed to demonstrate the presence, and to test the potency, of digestive enzymes are present in the pitcher fluid of all species of *Sarracenia*. In most it acts best in an alkaline medium, but in some acid is more favorable, as in the human stomach. Often it was found necessary to add an alkali (or an acid) to the pitcher fluid to obtain positive results. In any case, the several species differed greatly in the rapidity of digestion; in some it was swift but in others it

Purple pitcher plant or huntsman's cup, *Sarracenia purpurea*

required many days. Water and nitrogenous compounds released by digestion or decay are absorbed by the tissues at the bottom of the pitchers. Birds occasionally drink from them.

Also in the pitcher-plant family is *Darlingtonia*, with a single species, *californica*, in the north of that state and in adjacent southern Oregon, where it grows in swamps and on wet soil in open woodland glades. Springing from a perennial rootstock, the slender tubes, sometimes standing a yard high, are twisted over much of their length until the hooded top faces outward from the clump. From the downwardly directed mouth of the hood hangs a broad, forked, "fishtail" appendage, the inner face of which secretes much nectar to lure insects that crawl over it to the orifice. The green tube is veined with red; the hood and top of the tube are thickly dotted with whitish, translucent windows through which trapped insects might vainly try to escape until, exhausted, they fall into the depths. The absence of glands indicates that enzymes are not secreted to digest the many small creatures that die there. Substances released by bacterial decay are absorbed by the inner surface of the tube and help to nourish the pale green-and-reddish yellow flowers that rise above it on long scapes.

The third genus in the pitcher plant family, *Heliamphora*, was unknown until about 1840, when the explorer R. H. Schomburgk found *H. nutans* growing in a marshy savanna at an elevation of about 6,000 feet (1,830 m.) on Mt. Roraima in southern British Guiana (now Guyana). In the wettest spots on the cliffs and summit of the mountain, rosettes of foot-high (30 cm.) red-veined tubes with flaring mouths spring from stout rootstocks in wide, dense stands. Along the front of each tube are two wings, and from the summit rises a little appendage, called the spoon, much too narrow to keep out the frequent rains. As in the foregoing pitcher plants, nectar glands at the top attract insects, and downwardly pointing hairs direct them inward to a smooth and shining zone over which they slip to the depths of the vessel, where more such hairs impede their escape. As in *Darlingtonia*, digestive glands are absent here. The white or pale rose, petalless flowers are displayed high above the tubes on red-tinted stalks. Other species of *Heliamphora* grow on the *tepuis*, isolated table-mountains that rise into the clouds from the savannas of southern Venezuela. Some are shrubby plants up to four feet (1.2 m.) tall, with pitchers up to two feet (60 cm.) high. A peculiar feature of some of these pitchers is a pore about halfway up the front, which permits excess rainwater to flow out.

Cobra lily, *Darlingtonia californica*

Through the eastern tropics from northern Australia and New Guinea to Ceylon, the Seychelles Islands, and Madagascar, and from sea level up to 9,000 feet (2,750 m.) in the mountains grow about seventy species of pitcher plants of the genus *Nepenthes* in the family Nepenthaceae. Most are found on wet ground or in humid forests, growing as epiphytes or as lianas that climb high into trees from terrestrial rhizomes. Some of the vines are thick and strong enough for use in the construction of rustic suspension bridges. In addition to its ascending vine, *N. ampullaria* sends stout branches creeping over the ground amid mosses, where they may be traced for several yards by the dense clusters of pitchers strung along them. Other pitchers are displayed in the treetops.

The leaves of *Nepenthes* are of two kinds. Some consist of a simple blade with a midrib that projects from its tip as a tendril, much like that of *Gloriosa superba* in the lily family. Other leaves are more complex: the tendril, which may become quite long, bears a pitcher at its end. The morphology of this peculiar formation is puzzling, but it reminds me of the foliage of the shrubby *Codiaeum* that grows in our garden with leaves of two sorts. Some are simple, long, slender, red-and-yellow ribbons. In other leaves the ribbon is in two parts, separated by a slender stalk that resembles a petiole. The apical section of the leaf is peltate, with a short, upturned edge, the barest suggestion of a cup, inward from the attachment of the false petiole. Moreover, a slender "tail" projects from the upper face of the leaf, a short distance behind its apex. It requires no great imagination to derive a cup from a peltate leaf by the upward growth of the basal extension to catch up with the main part of the blade. On this view, the apparent leaf of *Nepenthes* would be a phyllode, or petiole with a leaflike expansion. The stringlike tendril would be a continuation of the petiole, and the pitcher at its end would be a modified peltate leaf. The pitcher's lid would correspond to the tail of the *Codiaeum* leaf.

Hanging at the end of a tendril, the pitcher turns sharply upward, as is necessary to hold its liquid. It may be long and slender or short and stout, the latter especially in terrestrial pitchers, which may differ in shape from aerial pitchers of the same plant. The vessel narrows toward the oblique mouth, which is surrounded, as by a collar, by a firm, T-shaped, transversely corrugated rim, from which an array of sharp teeth project downward into the cavity. Above the mouth, on a necklike extension, stands a lid, which in some species is broad enough to serve as an umbrella

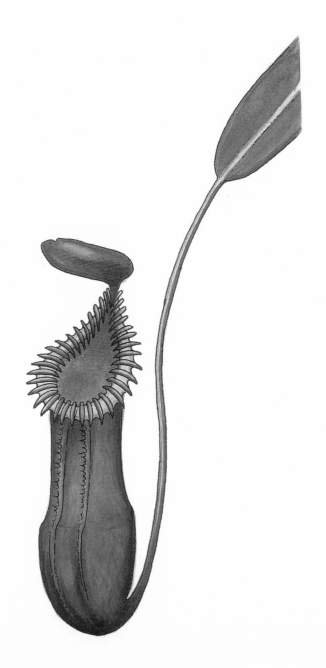

Nepenthes edwardsiana, a tropical pitcher plant

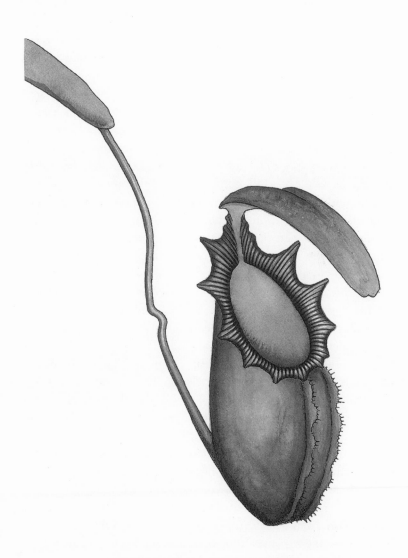

Nepenthes rajah, a tropical pitcher plant

over the pitcher. Some pitchers are big: one from Borneo measured eighteen inches (46 cm.) in length, including the lid. Its capacious bowl was large enough to drown a small mammal or bird. Along the pitcher's front are two wings, often with fringed edges. These vessels attract attention by their bright colors, red, claret, cream, or green, spotted or mottled with crimson, purple, or violet. Nectar glands on the leaflike basal expansion and on the tendril at its apex lure ants and other creeping creatures onward to the pitcher at the tendril's end, where they find more such glands on the underside of the lid and between the teeth on the inner edge of the collar. If from this point they venture inward, they find themselves on a glaucous waxy surface, the conducting zone, from which they slip into the depths of the trap, where they are surrounded by walls that appear to be both digestive and absorptive.

Until well grown, the bowl is tightly covered by its lid. This is not fused to it by growth, but the joint is sealed by dense branching hairs, like the wad of cotton in the mouth of a test tube. The closed young pitcher holds much secreted water, neutral and devoid of bacteria. In this watery grave small victims are digested by proteolytic enzymes poured out by the glands. To what degree they are supplemented by bacterial action it is difficult to learn. From pitchers heavily loaded with prey, odors of putrefaction arise, but these overfed traps might be said to suffer from indigestion. In addition to multitudes of ants, the *Nepenthes* pitchers capture centipedes, cockroaches, butterflies, large scorpions, and doubtless much else.

Pitchers of *Nepenthes* have given refreshing drinks to thirsty travelers, sometimes saving their lives. Alfred Russel Wallace (1872), who explored the Malay Archipelago in the mid-nineteenth century, found these plants most abundant in Borneo, where they flourished on every mountaintop, running over the ground or clambering over shrubs and stunted trees. He repeatedly expressed his admiration for the elegant pitchers of these "wonderful" plants, some of which hold up to two quarts of water. He told how, while traversing a hot, open, rocky slope high on Mt. Ophir in Malacca, he and his porters were overcome with thirst. Finding nothing better, they at last turned to the pitchers of plants that grew from fis-

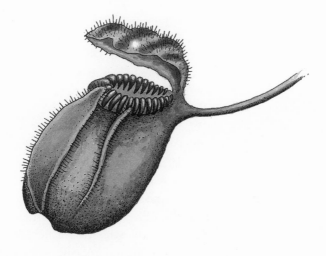

West Australian pitcher plant, *Cephalotus follicularis*

sures of the rocks, but were at first repelled by the many insects floating in them. Thirst overcoming squeamishness, they tasted the liquid, finding it very palatable but rather warm. All quenched their thirst from these natural jugs.

Australia, which supports more than its due share of unusual plants and animals, is the home of a curious little pitcher plant confined to a small region in the extreme southwest of the island-continent. From a taproot growing in drier parts of peaty swamps, *Cephalotus follicularis*, the only species in a family named for itself, produces rosettes of two quite different kinds of leaves, which alternate seasonally. The ovate foliage leaves, rarely more than five and a half inches (14 cm.) long, develop over winter and become full-grown in spring, then gradually wither, to be followed by the pitchers, which are well-developed and functional in summer, when insects are most abundant. Two inches (5 cm.) and often much less in length, each pitcher is attached to its stalk at the top, rather than at the base, as in all other pitcher plants. It has a wide, ridged lid, a corrugated rim, two wings along the front, and, below the down-ward-projecting teeth of the rim, a ledge extending around the inside with its acute edge jutting into the cavity, forming a kind of contracted neck. Small insects, mainly ants attracted by its nectar glands, fall into the bowl and are digested but, again, it is difficult to separate the effect of enzymes secreted by the pitcher from that of bacteria.

Very different from the foregoing passive traps are the ten species of *Genlisea*, which grow chiefly in Brazil, the Guianas, and Cuba, with two in western Africa. Although placed in the bladderwort family (Lentibulariaceae) on the basis of its floral structure, it is quite different, too, from the other genera in this family. All its species are small, rootless plants of swamps and marshes, where they grow in shallow water, with the inflorescences rising above it, as in the aquatic bladderworts. Like *Cephalotus*, *Genlisea* has two kinds of leaves: linear or spatulate foliage leaves and trap leaves, closely intermixed along a slender rhizome. In length these traps range from less than an inch (about 2 cm.) to four or five inches (10–12.5 cm.). From a tiny, bulbous base rises a long, slender neck, and at the open top of this little flask diverge two slender arms, each a ribbon folded into a tube and twisted into a spiral, those on opposite sides of the flask wound in opposite directions. The apposed edges of the ribbons are held apart by swollen cells placed at intervals, leaving between them funnel-like openings guarded by inwardly directed hairs. The tiny copepods, nematode worms, or spiders that venture through the funnels find themselves in a nar-row passage bristling, from the tips of the arms down through the neck to the bulbous bottom of the flask, with inwardly directed hairs arranged in transverse rows, and covered with mucilage from many glands. Whether these glands also secrete digestive enzymes appears not to be known, but victims only halfway down the neck are already well advanced in disintegration. These traps lined with inwardly pointing hairs have been likened to lobster pots or eel

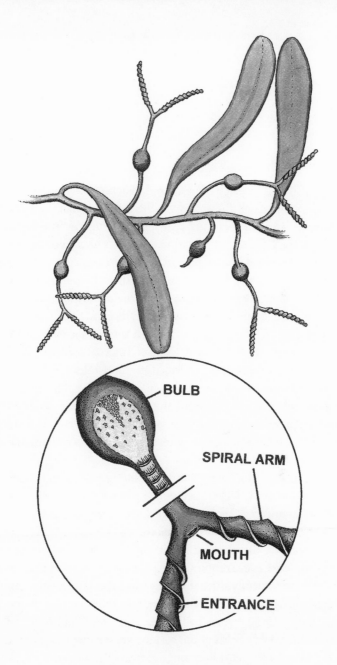

Genlisea sp., branch with foliage
and traps and details of trap enlarged

traps, which are crude structures in comparison to these marvelously complex little snares, perhaps the most intricate among all the carnivorous plants.

ADHESIVE LEAVES

Instead of pitfall traps or other closed structures, a number of carnivorous plants catch their prey on the exposed, sticky surfaces of their leaves. Among them are two species of *Byblis*, in a family of their own, the Byblidaceae, confined to western and northern Australia. The larger of them, *B. gigantea*, is a half-shrub up to twenty inches (50 cm.) high, which grows in the drier, better drained parts of sandy swamps. Arising from a slender rhizome, the sparsely branched stem bears linear leaves four to eight inches (10 to 20 cm.) long and, on stalks springing from their axils, violet or rose-colored flowers with five-lobed corollas. In cross section the leaves are triangular, with rounded edges. On the two lower sides of the triangle are many stalked glands that secrete abundant mucilage. The sessile glands on all faces of the leaf have a less viscous secretion that appears to be digestive, and they also give evidence of absorption, on the strength of which *Byblis* is included among the true carnivorous plants.

Not all plants with sticky glands to which small creatures adhere and die digest and derive sustenance from their victims; if they gain any benefit from their adhesive vesture, it is other than nutrition. In New Zealand grows a small tree of the four-o'clock family (Nyctaginaceae), the Parapara, with inflorescences so viscid that small birds and even reptiles that have the misfortune to touch them become so firmly stuck that they succumb. The Sleepy Catchfly in the pink family is so named because many insects die on its viscid glands. Other species of *Silene*, and the Clammy Cuphea that grows in weedy fields in the eastern and central United States, also detain small insects alighting upon them, but none of these plants is carnivorous. Neither is the shrubby *Roridula* of South Africa, once reputed to digest the creatures that stick to its glandular foliage. Similarly, insects that drown in rainwater that collects in the cupped leaf bases of Teasels and the Cup Plant do not nourish these tall herbs, which secrete no enzymes to digest them. These are a few of the many cases in which the structure or behavior of one organism is responsible for the deaths of many others from which it derives no benefit.

A viscid plant that does digest its captures is *Drosophyllum lusitanicum*, a relative of the sundews. Unlike the many carnivorous plants that prefer humid situations, this shrub, which resembles *Byblis*, grows on dry hillsides in Portugal, Spain, and Morocco, where its roots penetrate deeply into stony soil. It attains a height of six feet (1.8 m.) and displays large, bright yellow flowers. The long, narrow leaves bear glands of two kinds; stalked glands emerge from the edges and lower side; sessile glands are scattered over both surfaces, much as in *Byblis*. The former are hardly less complex than those of sundews but are not mobile; they secrete large droplets of clear mucilage that attract and hold many flies and other insects but do not digest them. On the capture of a victim, they send a stimulus to surrounding sessile glands, which thereupon secrete a pepsinlike proteolytic enzyme that can completely digest a fly in twenty-four hours, without the aid of bacteria. These same glands absorb the products of digestion, which compensate for deficiencies in the poor upland soils where *Drosophyllum* grows. In Portugal and Morocco, the plant is hung up in houses to catch flies.

About one hundred species of sundews of the family Droseraceae are widely distributed over Earth, with a preponderance in South Africa and Australia, where they exhibit the most diverse forms. Typically, a sundew has a perennial rhizome crowned by a rosette of glandular, round or elongate leaves, from the axils of which spring slender stalks that display white, magenta, purplish, or scarlet flowers. On some species the leaves are spoon-shaped; on others they are a foot (30 cm.) long and very slender; on some Southern Hemisphere sundews they are divided and fernlike. The yard-long, wiry stems of *Drosera gigantea* grow in dense tangles through which they twist and clamber, aided by certain long-petioled leaves, the blades of which become adhesive discs for attachment. Other leaves of this peculiar plant are peltate and deeply cupped. Sundews

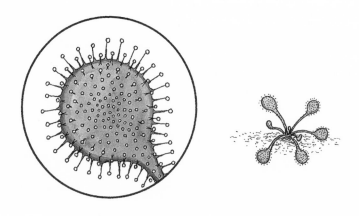

Round-leaved sundew, *Drosera rotundifolia*,
whole plant and a glandular leaf enlarged

are found mainly in places poor in nitrates and other soluble salts, the smaller species especially amid sphagnum, which during the cooler months grows more rapidly and covers the sundew, killing its leaves, whereas in warmer weather the latter rises above the moss to form a new rosette. The result is a succession of dead leaves clinging to the dead stem, which ends in a living rosette. Sundews draw attention by globules of mucilage that cover the upper faces and margins of their leaves and sparkle like dewdrops in sunshine. Each droplet is borne on and tinted red by a stalked gland of complex structure and diverse functions. It is not, like the hairs of plants and many of their glands, of epidermal origin but arises from deeper tissues. The multicellular stalk is traversed by spirally thickened conducting vessels, which lead to a knot of other conducting elements in the head, surrounded by three layers of cells, including the epidermis. In addition to mucilage, these glands secrete digestive enzymes and an acid antiseptic that prevents bacterial action, and they absorb the products of digestion. Fascinated by them, Charles Darwin (1875) gave to sundews more space in his book *Insectivorous Plants* than to any other genus and demon-strated their movements.

When, attracted by 130 to 250 glittering reddish droplets, a tiny insect alights on a short tentacle in the center of a leaf of the wide-spread Round-leaved Sundew and cannot free itself, this tentacle does not move but transmits to surrounding tentacles, as far as the leaf's margin, a stimulus that causes them to bend inward and apply their sticky heads to the struggling victim, binding it more firmly. If an insect is caught on a long outer tentacle, this sweeps inward to deposit the victim on short tentacles near the leaf's cen-ter, where it is joined by other tentacles. The rapidity of response varies with temperature and other factors; at best, movement visi-ble to the naked eye may begin ten seconds after a tentacle just within the leaf's margin is directly stimulated, and sweep through 180 degrees in twenty seconds, but usually it is much slower. After contacting the prey, the glands in the tentacles' heads pour out proteolytic enzymes to digest it, as revealed by changes in the pro-toplasm. The tentacles remain in contact with the corpse until all its nutriment has been extracted, which may take up to five days; then they separate and return to their original positions. The same tentacle may close upon three successive victims, after which its capacity for bending, which is effected by unequal growth of the sides of its stalk, appears to be exhausted.

The sundew's tentacles respond not only to insects or tiny par-ticles of food such as meat or cheese placed upon them but like-wise to stimulation without nourishment, as by stroking them gen-tly with a fine brush. Darwin was amazed to find that a fragment of soft thread only one-fiftieth of an inch long, or a much shorter particle of human hair, caused a tentacle to sweep through an angle of more than eighty degrees. After stimulation that yields no food, the tentacles bend outward again much more promptly than when they are fed. Experiments by Charles Darwin's son, Francis, and other investigators showed clearly that sundew plants nour-ished by insects are more vigorous, produce more and larger inflo-rescences, more seeds, and greater dry weight than those, otherwise similarly treated, that are prevented from catching prey. While the drosera plant digests the proteins of insects, it continues to carry on photosynthesis at a normal rate for its carbohydrates.

FOLDING LEAVES

From sundews we turn to another plant in the same family, Venus's-flytrap, which in an unguarded moment Charles Darwin called "the most wonderful plant in the world." At least it is unique, the only member of its genus, and with no remotely similar plant except *Aldrovanda vesiculosa*. *Dionaea muscipula*, as the flytrap is known to botanists, grows only in sandy bogs and wet pinelands in North and South Carolina. It is an inconspicuous herb that from a short rhizome produces at ground level a rosette of small leaves, from the center of which arises a long, leafless stalk crowned with a cluster of small white flowers. Each leaf consists of a petiole broadened into a green blade and, separated from this by a short slender stalk, the lamina divided into two lobes, or valves, that can fold together. Charles Darwin's grandfather, Erasmus, regarded this as a contrivance to protect the plant from insects by crushing or piercing any that might crawl over it. Actually, these leaves are not defensive but devices to snare, kill, and digest small victims. From the upper surface of each lobe spring three long, sensitive bristles, arranged in a triangular pattern. The rest of this surface is densely dotted with sessile glands, so numerous that their bright red color tinges the whole face of the leaf. From the margin of each lobe projects a single row of rather long prongs or teeth. When an insect alights on a lobe and bends the bristles on its upper side, the two lobes snap together, and the marginal projections, interlocking like fingers of our two hands, form a cage that confines larger insects, while tiny ones, hardly worth the expenditure of the plant's digestive juices, can escape through the bars.

Although structurally similar, the sessile glands on the leaf's upper surface have different functions. Just within the leaf's margin runs a band of alluring glands from which the secretion, apparently sweet, attracts ants and other small creatures; digestive glands, responsible for the leaf's red color, occupy the major part

Venus's-flytrap, *Dionaea muscipula*, plant
with traps open and closed on prey

of its upper face. When, after enjoying the exudate of the marginal glands, a small visitor moves farther inward, it can hardly
avoid touching one of the six bristles, each of which is a multicellular structure with, near its base, a transverse layer of sensitive
cells, where it readily bends. To spring the trap, the creature must
either touch the same bristle twice or each of two bristles once,
with an interval of no less than three-quarters of a second but no
more than twenty seconds. When stimulated in this manner, the
valves may, in optimal conditions, fold together in less than half a
second, although often the movement is much slower. It is effected,
not by a hinged midrib, but by the rapid stretching of the underside of each valve.

If the prey is appropriate, the valves tighten upon it and may
remain closed for from five to ten or more days, opening after the
corpse is fully digested, to become ready for another capture.
When the trap closes without prey, as it can be made to do by
mechanical or electrical stimulation, it reopens in about twenty-
four hours, to become again responsive. When an insect, a bit of

albumen, or some other source of protein is enclosed, the sessile glands pour out a proteolytic enzyme in an acid medium that inhibits bacterial action. The trap does not reopen until it is again dry, the glands having absorbed all the liquids. Wind blows away the insect's hollow exoskeleton. A trap may catch up to three insects, one at a time.

The only other species known to have a trap similar to that of *Dionaea* is *Aldrovanda vesiculosa* of the same family, a rootless aquatic sparingly found floating just below the surface of quiet acid ponds from southern France to Japan, Australia, and tropical Africa. It is an inconspicuous plant rarely over six inches long and somewhat less than an inch broad (15 by 2 cm.), which remains wholly submerged until it sends into the air short stalks with white flowers. Its slender stem bears closely spaced whorls of eight leaves, each of which consists of a broadly expanded petiole, much like that of Venus's-flytrap, bearing at its end a round blade and four to eight serrated bristles, which project beyond the general contour of the plant and impart a spiny aspect. On the concave upper surface of each semicircular half of the leaf, among the many glands that one expects on carnivorous plants, stand about twenty long, slender, multicellular hairs. Near the middle of each is a sensitive zone that corresponds to that of the more massive trigger-bristle of the flytrap. A light touch on one of these multicellular hairs often causes the valves of a young *Aldrovanda* to spring together like a mussel shell, but sometimes more touches are needed. Older leaves usually require greater stimulation than newly expanded ones. Although the traps appear capricious or unreliable, a tiny aquatic creature that swims among the crowded trigger-hairs will probably impinge upon enough of them to effect its own incarceration. After closure, the valves press their outer zones more firmly together, enclosing a little pocket in which the prey is digested and the products of digestion are absorbed. Then the trap expands to await another victim as, unless overfed, it may do repeatedly.

Thirty species of butterworts are distributed throughout the North Temperate Zone, reach the Arctic, and grow on high tropical mountains. In acid bogs, mossy banks, or damp crevices in stony outcrops, the perennial rootstocks bear compact rosettes of soft, fleshy leaves that usually press the ground or rock face. Their spurred flowers, borne singly on slender scapes, are white, yellow, blue, pink, or purple, often so large and handsome that they are cultivated as ornamentals. Some resemble violets. These plants of the bladderwort family receive their generic name, *Pinguicula* (from *pinguis*, fat), because the leaves of some are greasy to the touch. They are called butterworts apparently because the Lapps of northern Scandinavia pour the still-warm milk of their reindeer cows through sieves lined with these leaves, which contain a rennetlike substance that coagulates the milk into a sort of butter.

Pinguicula vulgaris, widespread in both Eurasia and North America, is the species in which Darwin first demonstrated the carnivorous habit of butterworts. Its ovate, entire leaves are thickly studded on the upper side with slalked glands that glisten with mucilage attractive to small flies. Between them lie more numerous sessile glands, the function of which is digestive. The margins of the leaf are incurved. When a little insect sticks to the mucilage glands toward the sides of a leaf, the edges slowly curl farther inward, bearing the captive toward the center and forming a broad and shallow trough that helps retain the liquids profusely secreted by the glands. These contain an enzyme that digests the victim, or almost any kind of protein placed upon the leaf, along with a weak acid disinfectant. The inrolling, which appears to leave the leaf's broad central zone uncovered, may continue for several days, after which, with the completion of digestion and absorption, the movement is reversed and the leaf flattens out again. Butterwort leaves can deal effectively with only very small insects, such as tiny flies; larger victims putrefy and damage the tissues. As a carnivorous plant, *Pinguicula* combines features of *Drosophyllum* and *Byblis*, in which glandular leaves attract and passively hold prey, and of *Dionaea* and *Aldrovanda*, in which leaves close over the booty much more swiftly and completely.

SUCTION TRAPS

The largest genus of carnivorous plants is *Utricularia*, the bladderworts, with about 275 species of worldwide distribution. In the North

Common butterwort, *Pinguicula vulagris*, flowering plant

Temperate Zone these plants float in still water, above which they lift only their flowers, or less often they grow on wet, sandy shores. Most widespread and familiar is the Greater Bladderwort, *U. vulgaris*, with rootless stems, up to a yard long, supporting leaves dissected into many capillary divisions that bear tiny bladders. Of the more numerous species in the tropics, some are aquatic like the northern forms but most grow as epiphytes on mossy trunks and branches, or on the ground, often amid mosses or humus in which their bladders are hidden. *U. nelumbifolia* flourishes in the aerial pools of rainwater caught in the tight rosettes of epiphytic tank bromeliads, spreading from tank to tank by means of runners. Two species, *U. neottioides* of Paraguay and southern Brazil and *U. rigida* of Africa, depart from bladderworts' preference for still waters by growing attached to rocks in swiftly flowing streams, in the manner of riverweeds of the family Podostemonaceae. Some epiphytic bladderworts store water for the dry season in tubers.

Wherever they grow, bladderworts most attract our attention when they send flowering stalks above the water or moss that covers them. In swamps of western Australia, long inflorescences of *U. volubilis* twine around supporting reeds. Some epiphytic species are so small and inconspicuous that they might never be found without the flowers that emerge from the moss in which they are embedded. Bladderwort flowers are white, yellow, blue, or purple. Some of the epiphytes have such large, beautiful blossoms that they are readily mistaken for orchids, which grow in the same places. Among the latter is *U. endresii* of Costa Rica, one of the more robust epiphytic bladderworts, which becomes fourteen inches (35 cm.) tall and bears lovely purple flowers, marked with yellow, an inch and a half (4 cm.) broad.

With one or two possible exceptions, all bladderworts bear the little utricles for which they are named. In length these closed vessels range from about $1/17$ to $1/5$ of an inch (1.5 to 5 mm.). Although they vary greatly in structural details, all appear to capture their diminutive prey in the same manner, by sucking them in, much as in a laboratory we pick up a tiny swimming creature in a pipette by permitting its flexible rubber cap to expand at the critical moment. To understand how this works, we must look closely at the structure of a trap, taking as our example the Greater Bladderwort. In warm weather the richly branched leaves of this plant become long, and at the height of summer two hundred of these little suction traps have been counted on a single large leaf, but this is an unusual number; only a dozen or so are more commonly found. About one-eighth

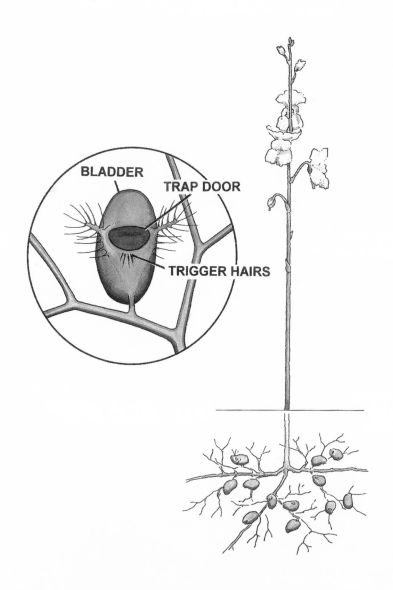

Greater bladderwort, *Utricularia vulgaris*, aerial
flowering stem and submerged leaves with bladders

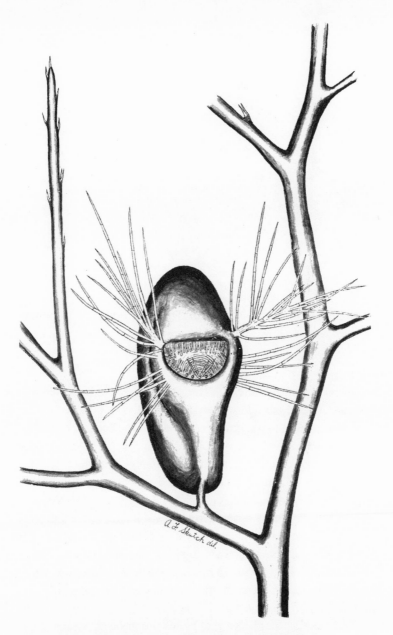

Greater bladderwort, *Utricularia vulgaris*, bladder
viewed from the front showing valve and appendages
around the orifice. From a drawing by the author.

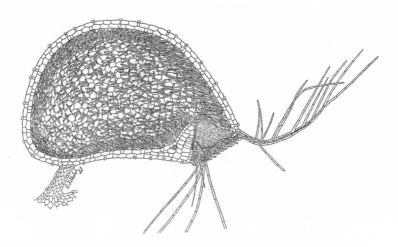

Greater bladderwort, *Utricularia vulgaris*, bladder with one side
removed to show internal structure. Drawing by the author.

of an inch (3 mm.) long, the bladder has a strongly arched dorsal
side and a nearly straight ventral side, to which is attached the short
stalk that joins it to a segment of the leaf. The mouth, or doorway,
at the other end, is directed obliquely downward. Its upper edge is
straight, its lower edge a semicircle. From each corner of the mouth
springs one of a pair of long, branched appendages, which Darwin
called antennae, from their resemblance to the antennae of a small
crustacean. From the sides of the mouth below these appendages
diverge a number of hairs, several cells long and one cell thick,
which may funnel small swimming or creeping creatures to the
entrance. The bladder's light green, translucent walls, only two cells
thick except where traversed by a vascular bundle along the top and
bottom, impart an aspect of delicacy.

The semicircular valve that closes the orifice is attached by its
straight upper margin and partly along the sides but free along its
curved lower edge, in the center of which it bulges outward. From
this convexity spring four bristles in two pairs, the triggers that
release the valve. Its unattached lower edge presses firmly against

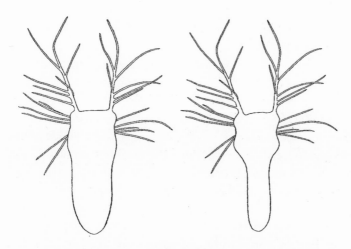

Greater bladderwort, *Utricularia vulgaris*, bladder set (right)
and same bladder expanded after touching valve
with needle. Camera lucida drawings by the author.

the thick, multicellular sill in such a manner that it can move inward
but not outward. A delicate membrane, called the velum, helps to
make the joint watertight. Glands that secrete a mucilage apparently attractive to animalcules thickly cover valve and sill. A small
creature entering through the door finds itself in a closed chamber
with walls covered with four-armed hairs, Darwin's quadrifids. The
outer or anterior pair of arms are directed more or less sideward,
while the longer posterior pair point inward. The latter are longest
at the entrance and become progressively shorter toward the bladder's stalk. This vessel's outer surface, like the plant's leaves and
stem, bears many glands with round, slightly projecting heads.

The traplike construction of the bladder is obvious. A small
aquatic creature, impinging upon the valve or its trigger hairs from
the outside, readily enters; but it cannot easily escape, for pressure
against the inside of the doorway pushes it more firmly against the
resisting sill. Apparently, it is all as simple as a cage rat trap, which
no one but the rat finds it difficult to understand. But why should

the animal enter the bladder, since no creature voluntarily incar-
cerates itself? The rat pushes into the trap for the bait; but what
within the sealed bladder can be sensed by an animal outside and
entice it to enter? This problem began to engage botanists after the
Crouan brothers, pharmacists and amateur botanists of Brest in
France, in 1858 communicated to the scientific world their discovery that the *Utricularia* bladders held imprisoned animalcules.
Before this, these vesicles, which when removed from the water
often contain much air, were believed to be floats to hold the inflorescences above the surface. A few aquatic species, including *U.
inflata* of the eastern United States and *U. stellaris* of Malaysia, have
at the base of the flower stalk a whorl of hollow, air-filled petioles
to sustain it, but other species lack such buoys. All parts of the
Greater Bladderwort and similar species are buoyant with air in
intercellular spaces, although their submerged trap bladders contain no air. The numerous epiphytic bladderworts certainly have
no need of floats.

Darwin was the first naturalist to consider seriously how and
why animals that are trapped in such large numbers enter the
bladders. In spite of prolonged and patient observations, which he
describes in detail in *Insectivorous Plants*, published in 1875, he failed
to reach a convincing explanation of how the trap works. He suggested that small creatures might be attracted to the bladder to
feed on the mucilage around the orifice, and might even "habitually seek to intrude themselves into every small cavity, in search of
food and protection," but he ends with the unsatisfactory conclusion that "animals enter merely by forcing their way through the
slit-like orifice, their heads serving as a wedge." And in the years
that followed, other able investigators endeavored to penetrate the
mystery of the bladderwort, with results equally inconclusive.

A MYSTERY SOLVED

About the year 1910, the Swiss entomologist Frank Brocher became
dissatisfied with Darwin's generally accepted explanation. Believing
that nobody had followed closely enough the entry of an animal into

a bladder, he decided to watch with great care. On the upturned surfaces of valves he pushed around small crustaceans, injured so that they could not too readily swim away, while he watched through a microscope. Sometimes they suddenly vanished, to be found later inside the bladder. Next he tried shooting these creatures against valves from a small pipette, usually with no enlightening result. Once, however, the animal disappeared into the bladder, and with it went a bubble of air to which it had become attached while in the pipette. This minute bubble was the key to the mystery; it told Frank Brocher that the bladder expands as it captures its prey.

Following this clue, he was able to observe that a bladder suddenly became distended when with a needle he touched one of the four bristles on the valve, or the valve itself near their bases. The impact of a small creature had the same effect. As it dilates, a bladder sucks in a current of water, and with it the animal that collided with the releasing mechanism. Darwin had come close to solving the riddle when minute fragments of blue glass that he pushed gently over the valve's surface suddenly vanished and were afterward found inside; as did his son, Francis, when tiny cubes of green boxwood were similarly engulfed.

Published in 1911 in a journal of small circulation, Brocher's discovery did not claim wide attention, with the consequence that the same observation was made independently thrice more before the bladderwort's secret became better known. In 1916, a youth of eighteen, C. L. Withycombe, noticed while watching bladders with a hand lens that they expand instantaneously while they engulf their prey. This was in England, while in India, at about the same time, another naturalist made the same discovery in a different way. While distributing for study by his class specimens of a *Utricularia* with exceptionally large bladders, T. Ekambaram (1916) heard crackling sounds, somewhat like the ticking of a watch, each time he lifted a spray from the water. He traced the sounds to the bladders, which expanded and sucked in air as they were drawn through the pond's surface film, and he recognized that this almost explosive dilatation was their method of capturing prey. As a bladder emerges into the air, the water's contracting surface film apparently moves the trigger bristles and springs the trap, which draws in air and becomes inactive.

Finally, in 1925, Professor R. W. Hegner of Johns Hopkins University, while studying the fate of minute protozoa trapped in the bladders, incidentally noticed that they capture animalcules by suction. While I was a graduate student in botany at the same university, Hegner interested me in the history of the bladderwort. I found that the expansion of the bladders was quite obvious—after one knew what to look for (Skutch 1928). Nevertheless, without this initiation, the bladderwort's secret was so carefully guarded that it escaped Charles Darwin himself, his botanist son Francis, and other competent observers—all of which makes an interesting minor episode in the history of science that seemed worthy of recounting here.

The independent discovery by four people in as many countries of how victims are sucked into the bladderwort's green charnels raised other questions: How does the bladder's rapid expansion come about? What is its mechanism? This problem was tackled with fruitful results by two German botanists, Edmund M. Merl (1922) and A. F. Czaja (1922), who made it clear that the release of the set *Utricularia* trap is not, like the closure of a Venus's-flytrap leaf or the flexure of sundew tentacles, effected by a sensitive motor organ but is more mechanical, like springing a mouse trap. Later, Francis E. Lloyd (1942), an English botanist resident in the United States and Canada, called attention to a final detail, the delicate membrane that seals the trap door. The elucidation of the bladderwort's activity has been a thoroughly international endeavor, as all good science should be.

To understand the operation of a *Utricularia* bladder, let us choose one that has just expanded and follow its subsequent behavior. After the entry of the first victim, the valve, helped by its outward convexity, springs forward against the sill—much as a piece of flexible cardboard, bent into half a cylinder and indented by a finger at its lower edge, regains its convexity the instant the finger is removed. The four-armed hairs that cover the bladder's inner wall continue to absorb from the cavity water that is excreted to the exterior, probably chiefly by the sessile glands on the outside.

Since water cannot enter the bladder through the tightly sealed orifice, as its volume is reduced the side walls are slowly forced together by the pressure of the atmosphere and the overlying pond water, just as our cheeks are pressed against our teeth when we close our lips tightly and suck air from our mouth. The indrawn walls are elastic and tend to expand, which would draw in the valve and admit more water if the outward bulge of the valve, pinched by the incurved walls, did not resist the excess pressure of the medium. Viewed from above, the bladder has become much thinner than when newly sprung.

If now, fifteen to thirty minutes after the snare made its last capture, a small swimming creature impinges against the valve or its bristles, the unstable equilibrium is upset. The seal is broken; the strained walls spring outward, as through the orifice they draw in a current of water that carries into the trap the ill-omened creature that sprang it. The whole process is so swift that it escapes the notice of excellent observers not prepared for it; one instant the animalcule is swimming against the bladder, the next it is beating against the prison walls in vain search for an exit from its death cell. Once inside, the animal usually dies, but often not until it has been for several days a prisoner. It is slowly digested by an enzyme so weak that some researchers failed to demonstrate its presence, then its substance is absorbed by the quadrifid hairs, while benzoic acid in the trap fluid prevents the multiplication of bacteria. The same bladder may be sprung repeatedly—up to fourteen times in three days—and resets itself each time in half an hour or less, even while digesting its latest booty, until a number of living, dying, and partly digested victims are simultaneously present.

A hole punched in the wall by a needle, or a hair inserted between the valve and the sill, permitting water to enter, prevents resetting of the trap, which remains permanently distended. Cold, heat, and moderate concentrations of a poison may prevent the resetting of a sprung bladder by inhibiting absorption of water from the cavity by active cells, but unless they destroy the turgor of the wall cells, they do not prevent the springing of a set bladder—all of which is evidence that this is a mechanical process effected by the release of tensions in the enclosing tissues. This conclusion is strengthened by the failure of electrical or chemical stimulation, which cause the sensitive leaves of *Dionaea* or *Aldrovanda* to close, to have a corresponding effect upon the bladders, which respond only to physical contact.

The bladderwort's prey includes almost any creature that swims in its native pond or ditch and is small enough to pass through the bladder's mouth. Various small crustaceans—especially copepods, ostracods, and cladocerans—eel worms, rotifers or wheel animalcules, and infusoria are frequent victims. Mosquito larvae are so often caught that bladderworts have been considered as a means of combatting these pests. Tadpoles are sometimes swallowed head-first; and newly hatched fishes that have the misfortune of becoming entangled among bladderworts may be seized by their heads, tails, or still-attached yolk sacs. Mosquito wrigglers and diminutive vertebrates too large to be sucked in all at once are held while the valve clamps down on them, sometimes firmly enough to prevent, or at least retard, the inflow of water while it is removed by the quadrifid hairs, with the result that these victims are drawn slowly inward until they are wholly immured and digested.

The number of small creatures held captive by a single plant at one time may be enormous. Part of a greater bladderwort with combined length of main stem and branches of seven feet (220 cm.) bore approximately 13,860 bladders. The number of small crustaceans in each of ten bladders ranged from six to twenty-two, with an average of twelve, whence it was estimated that this part of the plant contained about 150,000 of these animals, in addition to a multitude of organisms of other kinds. A century ago, M. Büsgen (1888) made a few experiments which showed that bladderworts in water with no lack of small animals grew twice as fast as those in water from the same source from which most had been strained.

The small minority of flowering plants that have become carnivorous belong to six families, with traps of diverse forms, which have apparently evolved independently no less than eight times. None has lost its chlorophyll and capacity to synthesize carbohydrates, which it supplements with amino acids derived from the digestion of small animals. These paradoxical plants combine animal and vegetable modes of nutrition. They appear to approach animals halfway, which prompts us to ask whether any animal takes a complementary course and develops chlorophyll to synthesize at least part of its carbohydrates, while it continues to eat plants or other animals. As far as I know, none does. The chloroplasts found in the bodies of a few animals belong to symbiotic algae, as in the Green Hydra, a small coelenterate widespread in pools.

A less-known example of such an association is the flatworm *Convoluta roscoffensis*, which lives on the beaches of Normandy, rising to the surface while the tide is low to permit the algae in its tissues to carry on photosynthesis in the sunshine, then retiring into the sand to avoid being washed away by the rising tide. The colorless newly hatched *Convoluta* eats with its mouth like other flatworms; but soon motile green algae invade its body; its mouth closes; its excretory organs degenerate; it becomes wholly dependent for nutrition upon its algal associates, which in turn appear to use its waste products as a source of nitrates. However, these plant-animals are not self-perpetuating organisms; the algae lose the ability to reproduce, with the result that each new generation of worms is infected by algae that have hitherto remained independent.

On the wider view, the chief interest of carnivorous plants is as examples of life's versatility, its improbable or paradoxical developments. The compromise of nutritional self-sufficiency to become partly dependent upon animal food has contributed little to the success of plants. The carnivorous species are a very minor component of the vegetable kingdom; their disappearance from Earth would hardly be noticed by anyone except a few botanists with special interests. Not by (so to speak) imitating one another but by stubbornly retaining the outstanding attribute of each—the synthetic capacity of green plants, the mobility of animals—do these two major branches of the living world enter into the most fruitful associations. By pollinating their flowers or dispersing their seeds, animals recompense plants for foods that sustain them. To this interchange of benefits we owe not only a large part of nature's beauty, including the loveliness of flowers and the brilliance of many birds and butterflies, but the integrity of biotic communities.

7

Three Biological Heresies

A science, like a religion, develops an orthodoxy, and those whose thought diverges from it become heretics. Although in the present age they are not likely to be burned at the stake or forced by torture to recant, they can be penalized in various ways. Editors of scientific journals may reject their contributions; reviewers censure their books; universities are reluctant to give them professorships. Nevertheless, the scientific heretics of one age may become the revered pioneers of a later age. When astronomical orthodoxy favored a geocentric universe, Copernicus was a heretic whose book was not published until he lay dying. When biological orthodoxy supported the fixity of species, Darwin was a heretic who hesitated to promulgate his theory of evolution until prompted to do so by receipt of a paper, expounding similar ideas, that Alfred Russel Wallace sent to him from the East Indies. Among the biological heresies of our day are anthropomorphism, teleology, and intergroup selection. Anthropomorphism makes unproved assumptions about the psychic life of animals. Teleology, the doctrine that nature strives toward predetermined ends or goals, is rejected because mutations are random and the agents of selection, chiefly predation, disease, starvation, and climatic extremes, care not at all for the welfare of a species. Intergroup selection is in disfavor because individuals, rather than families or groups, are primarily screened by natural selection.

ANTHROPOMORPHISM

Anthropomorphic means humanlike in form. Most of humankind's gods have been more or less anthropomorphic, often revoltingly so. In zoology, anthropomorphism is the ascription of human characteristics to animals. The literal meaning of the word, derived from the Greek nouns *anthropos* (human being, man) and *morphe* (form) would lead one to conclude that it refers to the physical configuration of nonhuman animals rather than to their psychic qualities. To point out that the bones of a bird's wing correspond closely to those of a human arm and hand is certainly anthropomorphism in this literal sense. Indeed, anatomists recognize a fundamental similarity in the skeletons of all terrestrial vertebrates. Nevertheless, biologists who emphasize these similarities are never accused of anthropomorphism in a depreciatory sense. Such resemblances provide the strongest evidence for the theory of evolution; to deny them is to undermine its foundations.

When we turn from the anatomy to the psychic life of animals, we find a very different attitude among biologists. To recognize physical resemblances is orthodox; to recognize psychic similarities, at least above such basic feelings as hunger, pain, and sexual desire, is heresy. Are we to conclude, then, that some extranatural agent implanted the human mind in a body that evolved from earlier vertebrate forms? Proponents of this dualistic view of human origin have not been lacking, but this is not biological orthodoxy. The more consistent view is that the human mind and body evolved together. Both our physical structures and our psychic traits have antecedents among animals less richly endowed.

The difficulty is that psychic states are not observable as bones and organs are. Aside from our individual selves, consciousness is always an inference, never a datum. We infer the feelings of those closest to us by certain overt signs, vocal, facial, behavioral; we cannot prove by scientific procedures that they feel. The more unlike ourselves another creature is, the more precarious our inferences from its behavior become.

Our imagination is limited by our experience. It is difficult for us to imagine any feelings, affections, or enjoyments that might give value to another creature's life wholly different from those that have enhanced our own. An animal's psychic state may differ in intensity or tone from ours, but it cannot be utterly unlike anything that we have felt without becoming inconceivable by us. Among the experiences that might enrich the life of one of the more advanced animals, including many birds and mammals, are pleasure in spontaneous activity, such as flying and soaring by birds, gamboling by quadrupeds, swimming by dolphins; the comfort of companionship in a perilous world; affection for mates, especially among animals continuously paired; emotional attachment to nests and dependent young; aesthetic response to beautiful colors and melodious sounds; a bird's delight in its own singing; the comfort of a snug dormitory nest on a chilly night; and in a small minority of birds, joy in a tastefully decorated bower. Since all such satisfactions are of sorts that from time to time many of us experience, they are in this sense "anthropomorphic." Unless we ascribe to nonhuman animals certain psychic states that make life worth living to us, as likewise such debilitating passions as fear, anger, and hatred, we must view their lives as emotionally blank, with no zest in living.

We cannot prove that nonhuman animals enjoy living, are emotionally attached to mates and young, or are attracted by beauty; we can only seek indications and weigh probabilities. But instead of stigmatizing—I almost wrote "vituperating"—as anthropomorphic the attempt to demonstrate humanlike psychic qualities in animals, we should welcome every indication of their presence and be grateful to naturalists who call attention to them. The probability that they occur should raise our estimate of the worth of animate life, making us feel less alone in a world overcrowded with organisms. If all nonhuman creatures are devoid of the psychic attributes called anthropomorphic, it follows that during the immense age before humans arose, no gleam of joy, no warmth of affection, nothing to give living intrinsic value brightened the existence of any of the myriad animals that swarmed over a hospitable planet. Devoid of anything that might give value to existence, Earth might as well have remained lifeless until the human lineage abruptly acquired the psychic qualities that enhance our lives. We cannot prove beyond all doubt that this was not true, but to affirm the continuity of development of both anatomical and psychic characters accords well with evolutionary theory.

TELEOLOGY

The second frequently condemned heresy is teleology, the doctrine that natural processes are directed toward ends, that nature is pervaded by purpose. Since we humans are so purposeful, we spontaneously ascribe purpose to the animals around us, and often to nature as a whole. Thus, teleology might be considered an aspect of anthropomorphism, the ascription of human qualities to non-human things. The teleological thought of early humans was firmly incorporated in religions that thrive to this day and was accepted by Classical philosophers. Aristotle (*Physics*, bk. 2, ch. 3) recognized four categories of causes: material, formal, efficient, and final. The first, or material, cause is the matter of which anything is made. The second, or formal, cause is the archetype or the form that it will assume. The third, or efficient, cause is the mover, or agent, that shapes the material into form. The final cause is the end for which the object is created, the goal toward which a movement is directed. To take one of the examples that Aristotle gives, the material cause of a bowl is the silver of which it is made. Its formal cause is its design, perhaps an image in the silversmith's mind, or a model that he copies. The efficient cause is the smith himself, who hammers it out with arms and hands. The final cause is the finished product, or the use for which it is intended. In general, the final cause is the end, for the sake of which something is made or done, as health is the end of the physician's art.

A complex artifact may have multiple causes: a variety of materials may enter into its construction; different components may be planned by different designers; many workers may be needed to make its parts and assemble them; if it can serve in diverse ways, it may be said to have several final causes in the Aristotelian sense.

Only efficient causes can accomplish ends. Unless it find means, a purpose is as helpless as a hatchling sparrow. To be effective, a final cause must find adequate material and efficient causes. An end capable of fulfillment becomes a selector of causes, itself a cause of the second order.

Modern technology is, of course, deeply concerned with final causes—the uses to which its inventions can be put, the profits they will bring to their manufacturers. Pure science concentrates upon the first two causes: matter and the forces that move or shape it. A form is viewed not as a cause but as a result of the action of forces upon matter. Final causes, ends for the sake of which things happen or are done, are commonly viewed as beyond the purview of science. This is true even in biology, which deals with the living world, where, if anywhere, we are inclined to look for purposes. Organs and tissues appear to be formed to serve definite ends; animals appear to act with a purpose. Since we are such purposeful, goal-oriented bipeds, our language is so rich in teleological expressions that young students in a biological laboratory do well to be careful how they use it. They will be safer from rebuke by a meticulous professor if they speak of the function rather than the purpose of an organ. The harmless little preposition "to" has teleological implications: we study to learn; we work to earn money. To avoid so much as a suspicion of this heresy, the student should say, "The plant grows upward and spreads its leaves in the sunshine," not "in order to spread its leaves . . . ."

A major concern of contemporary biologists is evolution. I infer from the titles of many papers that their authors believe it more important to know how an animal evolved (usually a speculative question) than how it lives and acts (which often can be learned by patient observation). In discussions of evolution—which to the naive onlooker sometimes appears to be directed toward ends— purpose, design, or goal are strictly taboo; only material and efficient causes are admissible.

Contemporary theory recognizes three major steps in the evolution of species. The first is mutation, resulting from alterations in the arrangement of molecules in the genes that jointly determine the forms, colors, functioning, and innate behavior of organisms. Genes are distributed along the strands of deoxyribonucleic acid (DNA), which together form the "coil of life." Mutations are demonstrably caused by hard radiations, certain chemicals, and thermal agitation of the molecules. Since their occurrence is random in the sense that they are not related to the needs of the organism, most of them prove to be harmful instead of beneficial.

The second step in the evolution of all organisms that reproduce sexually is recombination. In the formation of a germ cell—egg or sperm—the gene-bearing chromosomes, present in pairs in each parent's body, are separated randomly to form sets of unpaired chromosomes, thus halving their number. At fertilization, the set formed by the male parent is united with the set from the female parent in the nucleus of the egg cell, replicas of which the new organism will carry in all its tissues. The whole process is reminiscent of dealing out playing cards (Skutch 1985).

The third step in evolution is natural selection, which by agents the most diverse—malfunction of organs, climatic extremes, malnutrition, predation—eliminates individuals poorly endowed by the foregoing random processes, like unlucky gamblers who receive poor hands of cards. However, natural selection does not consistently remove the poorly adapted and preserve the fittest to survive. Accidents occur; a well-endowed animal may fall prey to a predator, while an inferior individual that happens at the moment to be better concealed escapes it. From first to last, and most strongly in the first two steps, chance enters largely into this schema of evolution.

It is easy to understand how mutation and recombination, continued through long ages, might cause the great diversity of the living world. Natural selection is essentially destruction; it eliminates the poorly endowed, while of promising mutants it takes no special care, such as an intelligent breeder of plants or animals gives to individuals that show improvement in the desired characters. Although an organism may be better equipped to resist the stresses or to profit from the opportunities a natural environment offers, the latter does nothing to favor the superior individual, as we might expect it to do if natural selection resembled the breeder's artificial selection, which is responsible for the misleading term. Although we detect nothing constructive in the orthodox account of evolution, when we survey its products, the plants and animals that fill the living world, their great diversity, their marvelous adaptations to the most varied situations, the beauty of many of them, the intelligence of some, we recognize that construction has occurred. Causes must be adequate to produce the results attributed to them. What is lacking in the above synopsis of evolution? Could it be a final cause, or a purpose? To answer this question, we must look closely at final causes, which imply ends.

Aristotle's dictum (*Physics*, bk. 2, ch. 8) that it is absurd to suppose that purpose is not present because we do not observe the agent deliberating becomes the more convincing the more we reflect upon our personal experiences. Sometimes, after trying through much of a day to find a solution to a perplexing problem, I have fallen asleep without reaching a conclusion. Next morning, I awake with the answer clearly in mind. If we insist that purpose is always a goal or end that we consciously try to attain, then purpose was absent while I slept. Nevertheless, it was then more effective than while I pondered my problem. Evidently, my purpose was not dormant even while I was unaware of it, but it had become implicit rather than explicit.

We are never more acutely conscious of our purpose than when we painfully learn to perform a difficult task. As we become expert and our activity habitual, our purpose appears to migrate from our minds to our muscles, which without conscious guidance repeat familiar operations. We might say, paradoxically, that we become less purposeful as we become more proficient. Moreover, all our consciously directed activities are supported by the autonomic functions of our bodies, including the pulsations of the heart, circulation of the blood, and metabolism, without which we can accomplish nothing. Our explicit purposes shade into implicit purposes in a manner that makes it difficult to separate them sharply; the distinction between them, although conceptually clear, is not profound.

Our conscious purposes are often directed toward ends that are optional, attainable by alternative routes, expertly or by trial and error. The vital physiological processes that support them require such precise and unremitting control that nature has not entrusted them to flickering consciousness, but the way they integrate with and support our conscious purposes points to a common origin, the purposiveness of life. Our strongest, most abiding purposes, our yearning for happiness, fulfillment, or a satisfying existence, appear not to be originated so much as discovered by us. Deliberation defines and directs strivings that rise from profound depths, the cosmic foundations of the living world. Only the more inconstant and trivial of our purposes appear to spring from a source no deeper than our conscious minds.

The constructive element we have been seeking in evolution, needed to complement mutation, recombination, and selection, appears to be of the nature of a final cause, an implicit purpose, the will of each creature to survive. It strives to make the best of its genetic endowment, however defective this may be, and to perfect itself according to its kind. The mutations it may have received were not designed to conform to its genetic constitution, but it adjusts them as best it can, like a mason fitting an oddly shaped tile into a mosaic. This will to grow and survive, however great the obstacles, is the only strong motive that we can detect in evolution. It is a phase of harmonization, the cosmic process that brings order into chaos, and in living organisms reveals itself most clearly as growth. This teleological movement is not directed toward specific ends, such as the production of a definite number of species of predetermined forms and attributes, but to the more inclusive end of increasing the organization of the cosmos and the values that arise from harmonious integration. The details are determined by the interplay of physical forces and the interactions of organisms.

A teleological impulsion might pervade the world without becoming explicit in the minds of animals. We often wonder how far they are aware of the ends of their activities. Does a bird, for example, build with a mental image, innate or learned, of the nest she is trying to complete? Is she conscious that she is making it for eggs and nestlings? I believe that she does and is, and that other highly organized animals are cognizant of the ends of at least the more elaborate of their activities; but I can offer no proof beyond inferences from their behavior. But neither can those who declaim against teleological interpretations of nature and animal behavior prove that I am wrong. Pending greater insight, we should keep our minds open while we hold, tentatively, the more generous interpretation.

Much of the opposition to the teleological interpretation of nature, or at least certain of its aspects, appears to spring from the practice (approved by Webster's dictionary) of using "purpose" and "end" as synonyms, and of equating teleology with conscious purpose. We should pay attention to the sentence from Aristotle's *Physics* already quoted. I do not know how it may be in the original Greek, but I surmise that the translation would more accurately convey the philosopher's meaning if we wrote: "It is absurd to suppose that a process is not teleological (or directed toward an end) because we do not detect a purpose," meaning by "purpose" a conscious intention, by "end" the result of a process or movement. The consistent use of "purpose" for consciously intended results, and of "end" for the result of a process, whether intended or not, would be conducive to clarity and make a teleological worldview more acceptable. "End" is the more inclusive category. All purposes, except possibly the most trivial, are directed toward ends, but not all ends are consequences of foreseeing purposes. Flowering is the end of a plant's growth, a teleological process, but not its purpose, unless we attribute thought to vegetation. Pervaded by harmonization, the cosmos has ends (possibly an inclusive end) but not purposes, except in the restricted areas where we can detect, or infer, the presence of foreseeing minds, as in humans and probably the more intelligent animals.

In a critical chapter on "The Multiple Meanings of Teleological," Ernst Mayr (1988) threw new light upon this difficult subject. In the programmed processes of organisms, which he calls "teleonomic," the great philosophical evolutionist recognizes "the teleological aspect of the living world." He tentatively defines "program" as "coded or prearranged information that controls a process (or behavior) leading it toward a given end." A program includes not only the blueprint but also the instructions of how to use the information it contains. Programs may be minutely detailed, as appears to be true of those that control embryological development, or open, subject to modification by learning, experience, or insights, as in the overt behavior of animals, or the more intelligent of them. These teleonomic programs are encoded in the DNA of the nuclei, where over the generations they were evolved, in relation to the organism's structure and needs, by the usual processes of mutation and selection. According to this interpretation, nest building, incubation, and other parental activities of a bird are details of a teleonomic process, the end of which is the rearing of fledglings. The southward migration of a northern bird in autumn is likewise teleonomic, to avoid the rigors of a cold winter. These and similar activities do not necessarily involve conscious purpose or foresight; but as some are demonstrably improved by learning, foresight might not be absent.

Although, not without opposition, liberal-minded biologists attribute a degree of teleology to the living world, its ascription to the cosmos as a whole is vehemently rejected by many contemporary philosophers and especially workers in the physical sciences. Nevertheless, I believe we may recognize in inorganic nature something analogous to the programmed activities of organisms. Atoms are social beings with strong tendencies to join others. Their sociality is of two kinds, undiscriminating and discriminating. The former is manifest in gravitation, which, aided by the medium that contains them, space, draws them together in great masses, irrespective of their kinds, and with an intensity determined only by the magnitude of these aggregations—the greater the crowd, the more eagerly the atoms appear to join it.

The discriminating sociality, sometimes called "chemical affinity," impels atoms to unite closely with certain other atoms or combinations of them, while avoiding union with others. Operating on a grand scale, the undiscriminating sociality of atoms condenses vast clouds of cosmic gasses and dust into stars, planets, and their satellites. Only on the surfaces of some of these planets, neither too hot nor too cold, enveloped in an atmosphere neither too dense nor too rare, can atoms give full play to their selective sociality, forming a great variety of salts and crystals and, in a watery medium, the very complex molecules of living organisms.

The social atoms unite in formation of increasing amplitude, complexity, and coherence—the process of harmonization. Among those of greatest complexity are the strands of DNA that form the coils of life, which encode the programs for the teleonomic processes and activities of organisms. We may trace a continuous progression from the union of atoms in the simplest molecules to the much more complex molecules of organisms. If the activities of these creatures are teleonomic, the movements of the social atoms seeking companions must be regarded as teleonomic in the same sense. One continuous movement runs through the universe from its prime foundations to its most advanced formations. It is improbable that creatures so purposeful as we humans, composed of atoms widespread in the cosmos, activated by the same energy that courses through it everywhere, arose in a universe devoid of teleology.

Nevertheless, the programs encoded in the genes of organisms and that implicit in the sociality of atoms differ greatly. The former, products of a long evolution, are highly detailed, differ from species to species, and are probably rarely exactly the name in two individuals who are not identical twins. Atoms appear to be coeval with the universe and their nature never changes. Their sociality determines only the general course of cosmic development, from the chaos of diffused cosmic dust to planetary systems of quite definite forms and movements, and on some planets a vast diversity of living creatures, whose forms and activities were not predetermined but resulted from their interactions with the lifeless and living components of their different environments, depending much on the chances of mutation.

As to the end or goal of the cosmic process, it appears to be to give value to the universe. No matter how vast its spread, how many millions or trillions of galaxies or stars it contained, a universe with no single being to enjoy its existence would, it seems, be so utterly valueless that nothing of importance would be lost if it were annihilated, leaving only nothingness. The cosmic process is best interpreted as an aeonian striving to increase the value of the

universe by producing creatures capable of enjoying their existence in it, but unhappily not without much suffering along the
way. And this striving or seeking for value or significance appears
to be a teleonomic process, programmed, in its general direction
although not in its details, by the sociality of the atoms.

An objection to the view that the universe is programmed to
augment its value by producing creatures able to enjoy their lives is
that, on present evidence, life is so thinly scattered through its
immensity. Of the nine planets in our solar system, only Earth is
known to support organisms, and billions of years passed before
some of them rose to the psychic level of aesthetic appreciation
and thirst for understanding. An answer to this objection is that a
universe that is apparently eternal and possibly of infinite extent
has unlimited time to create, by slow evolution, beings with an
advanced psychic life, and abundant resources to form millions of
planetary systems, so that a few of them might give birth to living
creatures. Possibly the atoms are not devoid of a degree of feeling
proportionate to their minute size and intensified and diversified as
organization increases. The two-aspect or bipolar ontology, which
I regard as the most satisfactory solution of the ancient problem of
the relation of mind to matter, postulates that every particle has a
physical side, public and the object of scientific study, and a psychic side, which like our own consciousness is private and unob-
servable by others. When the sentient atoms are arranged in a special pattern, as in a brain, consciousness is intensified and the more
advanced manifestations of psychic life develop. Although the
foregoing solution of the basic problem of teleology has much to
recommend it, we cannot prove it. Despite all our science and all
our philosophy, the universe guards its secrets well.

If we insist that teleology implies a conscious purpose widely
diffused through the universe, we are on precarious ground; when
we recognize a movement to increase the value of the cosmos, we
are on firm ground, for this is what it demonstrably accomplishes,
at least on Earth. The definite, consistently followed direction of a
teleological process distinguishes it from random movements.

I would not conclude from this that biologists should be concerned with teleology and give more attention to final causes: to elucidate the material and efficient causes that have shaped and preserve organisms should keep these scientists sufficiently busy. The investigation of final causes is more pertinent to philosophy than to science. But scientists should be more tolerant of philosophers' often groping efforts to throw light upon obscure aspects of reality that since people became thoughtful they have most ardently wished to illuminate; just as philosophers should be tolerant of the sometimes illogical pronouncements of scientists.

INTERGROUP SELECTION

The third of the most frequently condemned biological heresies is intergroup selection, often more briefly called "group selection." The orthodox view is that the natural selection of individuals, or their differential survival and reproduction, is adequate for the theory of evolution, or, more succinctly, that individuals rather than groups are selected by natural agents. This insistence upon the adequacy of interindividual selection has three weaknesses: it exaggerates the self-sufficiency of the individual, it neglects social interactions, and it underestimates the complexity of evolution—it is too simplistic.

Solitary animals, which associate with other adults only long enough to inseminate them or to be inseminated by them, are self-sufficient as to their survival but not as to their reproduction. Modern evolutionists assess the fitness of an organism by the number of its progeny; but no individual of a species that can reproduce only sexually is, in a strict logical sense, fit by this measure. It becomes fit only by choosing a partner in reproduction. Since each parent contributes an approximately equal number of genes to the progeny, the innate quality of the offspring, or their ability to survive and reproduce, will depend equally upon the genetic contributions of the parents, and their number will depend upon the adequacy of the parent contributing most to their production and nurture—usually the female, although in a number of species the male contributes substantially to the care of his offspring, and in certain birds, amphibians, and fish he is largely or wholly responsible for protecting and/or feeding them. This is the primary reason why insisting upon the adequacy of individual selection is an oversimplification of the problem of evolution. As though recognizing this, birds, more than most other animals, tend to be careful in the selection of their partners.

When we trace a lineage backward in time, we find that, in the absence of inbreeding, the number of ancestors increases geometrically with the number of generations—four grandparents, eight great-grandparents, and so forth. Each of these forebears has contributed genes, which jointly determine the quality of the latest progeny; all are virtually involved in their birth. Likewise, when we project the transmission of an individual's genes forward through its descendants, we find that they tend to diffuse ever more widely through a population. The individual that succeeds in reproducing is but a link in a lengthening chain. Without the opportunity to mate with enough unrelated individuals to prevent deleterious inbreeding and to provide the genetic diversity that is the foundation of adaptability, a lineage may become extinct. When a dwindling species or race is tardily given protection from humans and encouraged to increase, as we might expect it to do rapidly because of reduced competition for resources, it sometimes fails to recover but continues to decline, as happened to the Heath Hen on Martha's Vineyard, an island off the coast of Massachusetts. Lack of genetic diversity was one of the factors adduced for its extinction.

The perpetuation of an interbreeding population, its capacity to evolve or to extend its range, depends upon its gene pool, the aggregate of genes of which every individual bears a selection but none the whole range of them. In contemporary ornithology the term *cooperative breeders* is applied to a group consisting of a reproductive pair with one or more nonbreeding helpers. In a wider sense, all the members of an interbreeding population, or deme, form a single cooperatively breeding group, providing its progeny with mates, preventing debilitating inbreeding by exchanging genes. The number and quality of an individual's offspring—its fitness— depends upon the quality of the partner in reproduction that the species can provide for him or her.

Interindividual selection helps to maintain, or to improve, the anatomical and physiological quality of a species by removing, by agents the most diverse, defective or substandard individuals. It is adequate to account for the extinction of races or species. In the absence of a natural catastrophe that wipes out a whole population at a stroke, or a drastic climatic or ecological change that extinguishes it, individuals may be eliminated one by one, by predation, disease, or other natural agents, if not by humans, until the last member of a species vanishes from Earth. But individual selection cannot account for the evolution of a race, which depends upon changes in the composition of its gene pool, a process in which many interbreeding individuals participate but to which none can contribute alone.

The foregoing considerations apply to all organisms, plants as well as animals, that can reproduce only by the union of two individuals, or of their sexual cells, their gametes. In certain special situations, it is more obvious that evolution depends upon coordinated genetic changes in interacting individuals. The first is in the field of social relations. Animals attract sexual partners by signs or signals, which may be visual, vocal, olfactory, or a combination of these. If a mutation in the appearance, sounds, or odors of one sex is not supplemented by a complementary mutation in the preference or reaction of the opposite sex, the former will fail to mate and leave progeny, with the result that its mutation will disappear from the gene pool. The gorgeous plumage of many male birds, which since Darwin has been attributed to sexual selection, could not have developed if the preferences of females had not evolved in the direction of the changes of the males' attire. Cooperation of a male and female in rearing their young, the two sexes playing complementary rather than identical roles—as in many birds and fewer mammals—could hardly have been perfected without coordinated evolution in an interbreeding population. The calls or other signals by which animals alert their companions to approaching danger would be meaningless if signal and response did not evolve together in a group of related animals. Releaser and innate releasing mechanism, social interactions the most diverse, point to the natural selection of groups as well as of individuals.

In recent decades ornithologists have been discovering an increasing number of avian species that breed in closely knit groups of parents and their self-supporting offspring, who aid their elders in defending the territory, feeding and protecting their younger siblings, and often, too, in building the nest and incubating the eggs. Sometimes the family is joined by individuals less closely related. Some of the species in which cooperative breeding is widespread can breed successfully as unassisted pairs; others cannot. Among the latter are White-winged Choughs in Australia, Yellow-billed Shrikes and apparently also White-browed Sparrow-Weavers in Africa, in all of which pairs without helpers raise so few young, or suffer such high mortality, that their species would become extinct in the absence of cooperative breeding (Skutch 1987). In these cases it is especially clear that the unit of selection is the cooperating group; or, in terms of fitness, we might say that the fitness of an individual is strictly dependent upon its membership in a group.

The prominence given to individual selection in contemporary discussions of evolution, the widespread rejection of group selection, ignore the significance of sexual reproduction. The genes of an individual lack evolutionary importance unless they are contributed to the gene pool of its species; and the first step in this incorporation is their mingling with the genes of a second individual. The pair rather than the individual appears to be the primary unit of selection that does not lead to extinction, but this is only a step toward the wider diffusion of its genes through a larger group of interbreeding organisms. The sharp distinction between individual selection and group selection erects an artificial boundary in a continuum. Natural selection has both a negative and a positive aspect. It acts like a sieve, which holds back, for rejection, coarser particles, while permitting the finer grains to pass—finer, in the present context, meaning fitter or more adequate to confront their environment. And these finer individuals gain their evolutionary significance by mingling their genetic endowments with those of their contemporaries.

For examples of pure individual selection, we must turn to organisms that reproduce with never the intervention of sex. Their progeny form clones, all of whose members bear precisely the same constellation of genes, so that differences in their survival must be attributed to external factors instead of intrinsic differences. When feasible, horticulturists and agriculturists frequently prefer vegetative propagation, which is often quicker and more efficient than reproduction by seeds, and has the great advantage that plants so multiplied nearly always "breed true." Many of the most valuable agricultural plants, including potatoes, cassava, sugarcane, and bananas, are regularly propagated by vegetative parts; some of their varieties never set seed. Occasionally by a "sport," or bud variation, one of these cultivars produces a new and valuable variety, which must be propagated as a clone by vegetative means.

Despite the vigor of many plants that can reproduce only asexually, they rarely spread widely without our help; most would probably become extinct without human care. Among vertebrate animals, parthenogenesis is rare. Why has sexual reproduction, indirect and frequently wasteful, become so much more widespread among all the more highly evolved plants and animals than the more direct and efficient methods of asexual multiplication? The reason appears to be that strict individual selection does not produce the genetic diversity that promotes adaptability to confront changing conditions and the capacity for continuing evolution. Sexual reproduction and group selection have evolved because they promote evolution.

Darwin was aware of the inadequacy of individual selection. In *The Origin of Species* he wrote: "I did not appreciate how rarely single variations, whether slight or strongly marked, could be perpetuated." Farther along he elaborated: "But in the great majority of cases, namely, with all organisms which habitually unite for each birth, or which occasionally intercross, the individuals of the same species inhabiting the same area will be kept nearly uniform by intercrossing; so that many individuals will go on simultaneously changing, and the whole amount of modification at each stage will not be due to descent from a single parent." And again: "Hence in order that a new species should suddenly appear . . . , it is almost necessary to believe, in opposition to all analogy, that several wonderfully changed individuals appeared simultaneously within the same district. This difficulty . . . is avoided on the theory of gradual evolution, through the preservation of a large number of individuals, which varied more or less in any favourable direction, and of the destruction of a large number which varied in the opposite manner."

In these days when biology has become highly mathematical, the views of mathematical evolutionists have great weight, despite their disagreements. Many years after Darwin, Sewall Wright (1949) concluded that the subdivision of a species into partly isolated groups, or demes, between which there is limited interbreeding with resultant flow of genes, "provides the largest store of variability both locally and within the species as a whole, and by providing for selection in which whole genetic complexes are the objects, frees evolution most completely from dependence on rare favorable mutations and makes possible the most rapid exploitation of an ecologic opportunity." Elsewhere Wright (1940) wrote: "A local population that happens to arrive at a genotype that is peculiarly favorable in relation to the general conditions of life of the species . . . will tend to increase in numbers and supply more than its share of migrants to other regions, thus grading them up to the same type by a process that may be described as *intergroup selection*."

Another mathematical evolutionist whose writings are often quoted, R. A. Fisher (1958) denied the effectiveness of group selection, even in humans, who for ages lived in small, mutually hostile groups to which Wright's model might apply, and until quite recently continued to exist in this manner in vast areas of Amazonian forests. "The selection of whole groups," he wrote, "is, however, a much slower process than the selection of individuals, and in view of the length of the generation in man the evolution of his higher mental faculties, and especially of the self-sacrificing element in his moral nature, would seem to require the action of group selection over an immense period." In answer to this objection, we might remember that the evolution of man from prehuman hominids required at least two million years, or about a hundred thousand generations. Until modifications that spring up in individuals become firmly established in a population, however long this might take, evolution has not occurred. Fisher denied that "the principle of Natural Selection" affords a rational explanation "for any properties of animals or plants which, without being individually advantageous, are supposed to be of service to the species to which they belong." This is no argument against group selection, which does not require self-sacrificing activities but rather cooperation that benefits all participants, as in mutual defense, the search for food, the construction by groups of avian apartment houses in which many individuals nest and sleep, cooperative breeding, and among plants that grow gregariously, the maintenance of a habitat or microclimate in which they thrive better than when growing alone. Moreover, as pointed out in chapter 2, reproduction itself entails a sacrifice of the individual for the benefit of its species.

Group selection may transcend specific boundaries. The group favored by selection may consist of animals of two kinds that become mutually dependent, or of an animal and a plant, as occurs when a flower becomes specialized for pollination by one species of insect or bird, which in turn becomes highly modified for extracting nectar from that particular kind of flower. Unless the modifications of pollinator and flower keep pace with one another, such coevolution could not occur.

An inappropriate term can cause widespread confusion. Impressed by the results of human selection of domestic animals and plants, Darwin chose the term natural selection for a superficially analogous process in wild nature. Artificial selection and *natural selection* differ profoundly. An intelligent breeder of plants or animals takes special care of individuals that vary in a desired direction; nature does nothing of the sort—without pampering the more fit, it ruthlessly eliminates the less fit. Not surprisingly, many of Darwin's early critics (like not a few later ones) were perplexed by the term *natural selection*. On 6 June 1860, the year after the publication of *The Origin of Species by Means of Natural Selection: Or the Preservation of Favoured Races in the Struggle for Life*, he wrote to his friend, the geologist Charles Lyell: "I suppose 'natural selection' was bad term; but to change it now, I think, would make confusion worse confounded." On 26 September, he confided to the botanist Asa Gray: "If I had to write my book again I would use 'Natural Preservation' and drop 'selection'" (Burkhardt et al. 1993). The substitution of "natural preservation" for "natural selection" might have precluded the stubbornly short-sighted insistence that natural selection is confined to individuals, because it is undeniable that groups, species, and larger categories of organisms are preserved along with the individuals that compose them.

Happily, as the behavior of animals is studied more deeply and perceptively, as more and more examples of cooperation among them are disclosed, as the coevolution of animals and plants is investigated, the attitude of the biological community toward some of the heresies appears to be softening. It is beginning to be realized that the gap between human emotions and those of other animals need not be as wide as that in their intellectual development. It is becoming apparent that the selection of individuals is only the first step in an extremely complex process that extends to groups of individuals and finally to whole species, and even to two or more mutually dependent species. When we recognize the continuity of development from lifeless matter through all stages of evolving life, we may finally perceive that purposeful activity is not confined to humankind. We may even go beyond this to recognize that, in postulating a teleological universe, Aristotle, the first great naturalist-philosopher of whom we have knowledge, was not wholly wrong.

8

Biodiversity or Biocompatibility?

Many years ago, I established a homestead beside a large tract of tropical rain forest, in a region still wild. Around my new dwelling, I planted fruit trees and shrubs with colorful flowers, to provide nectar or berries for birds, and daily placed bananas for them on a board in a tree. Soon many, from the adjoining woodland as well as those of open country, nested around my house. With the troublesome exception of the nest-stealing Piratic Flycatcher, all dwelt peaceably together, singing their songs and rearing their young. But predators, chiefly snakes, small mammals, and an occasional raptor, invaded the garden to capture the adults or plunder their nests.

What should I do about this distressing situation? I believed that I owed protection to the birds that I encouraged to nest near me. After much thought, I adopted the principle of harmonious association. I would do all that I could to protect the creatures that dwelt harmoniously together, taking measures to remove those that disrupted this concord. For the adjoining forest, I preferred the principle of *laissez-faire*, or refraining from meddling with nature. Although the situation there, where predators abounded, was not ideal, it appeared too big and complex to be controlled by me, or by anyone.

Today, half a century later, humans have increased so greatly, and made their presence felt so widely, that the situation nearly everywhere is becoming more like that in farmlands and gardens than in wild, undisturbed woodland. During the same interval, the conservation movement has grown much stronger, notably in tropical countries where it was weak. Other than that all true conservationists try to preserve some part of nature, and beyond general agreement that the protection of habitats is indispensable, a wide diversity of preferences is evident among conservationists. Some are more concerned about forests, others about wetlands or oceans. Some are interested mainly in a special group of animals—birds or bats or amphibians. Some try to protect or increase raptorial birds, while others deplore the decline of birds on which raptors prey. These divergent aims sometimes clash, with the consequent waste of effort and of the inadequate funds available for the protection of nature. We must clarify our aims; we need a comprehensive goal for conservation.

As a guiding principle for conservation, the following alternatives are worth considering. We should endeavor to promote: (1) maximum diversity, or number of species; (2) the maximum sustainable number of individual organisms; (3) those elements of the natural world that contribute most to human prosperity and happiness or are the least threat to these ends. Let us examine them in this order.

"Biodiversity," a neologism, has become the rallying cry of conservationists. That we could not survive without biodiversity, and a great deal of it, is a truth too obvious to naturalists to need elaboration. We need plants to produce food; insects, birds, and other creatures to pollinate their flowers; fungi and microorganisms to decompose dead tissues and return their fertilizing components to the soil; and much else. Recent explorations of the canopy of tropical forests have revealed that the number of extant species is much greater than we had supposed only a few decades ago and may run into millions.

Biodiversity has certainly become excessive, and is responsible for a major part of the sufferings of animals, including humans. In addition to all the predators that strike down living victims and too often begin to tear them apart before they die, an immense diversity of parasites torture, debilitate, and kill their hosts. Since most multicellular animals appear to be infected by several kinds of parasites, internal and external, many of which are restricted to a single species or closely related group, it is probable that parasites far exceed, in number of species and individuals, all other Metazoa, or multicellular animals. Moreover, they can weaken and kill plants or ravage whole forests. Undoubtedly, a great reduction of biodiversity, probably 50 percent or more, would make life much more pleasant not only for humans but for many other creatures.

Although we hear much about biodiversity, I am not aware of any widely accepted statement of its desirable limits. Should we promote the absolute maximum, which would include all parasites, pathogens, and predators, or should we be more discriminating? I doubt that any advocate of biodiversity would oppose the extermination of organisms responsible for human diseases, or of the blood-sucking insects that spread diseases and can make life miserable for many kinds of mammals. In regard to larger predators, the situation is confused. Many friends of animals would welcome the great reduction, if not extinction, of venomous and nest-robbing snakes, voracious alligators, the fiercer raptors, or the most dangerous sharks. If conservationists could agree on the desirable limits of biodiversity, cooperation and efficiency might increase.

Instead of promoting biodiversity absolutely or within certain well-defined limits, we might choose the alternative of making our goal the maximum number of individuals, of all kinds or of certain specified kinds, within the capacity of Earth to support them indefinitely in a flourishing state. The contrast between the first and second alternatives presents an interesting analogy to that between two opposing principles of human government. Totalitarians hold that individuals exist for the wealth, power, and glory of the state, which certain philosophers, such as Hegel, have viewed as having a collective spirit or soul, above that of its inhabitants, and which can demand their sacrifice for the exaltation of the whole. Liberal democrats believe that the state, devoid of a collective spirit, exists for the welfare of individuals, who alone enjoy and suffer.

Similarly, advocates of unlimited biodiversity might view the global community of animals and plants, or perhaps the planet itself, with all its living cargo, as a superorganism, Gaia, which thrives most grandly the more species of all kinds, as well as individuals, it supports. Opposing this view, we might remember that we lack evidence of consciousness, or the capacity to suffer and enjoy, except in individual organisms. Accordingly, a liberal, compassionate conservation movement should be concerned with the welfare of individual animals rather than the entire biological community regarded as a mystic whole, and of individuals rather than of species. Some humanitarian philosophers, like Tom Regan (1983), maintain that every member of a thriving species has no less claim to our forbearance than have the few surviving individuals of a vanishing species. Thus, we may recognize a holistic or "totalitarian" approach to conservation, and an individualistic or "liberal" attitude.

A third alternative arises: widespread is the belief that we should protect the natural world, not for its own sake, but for its importance to humankind. Vegetable and animal species favorable to human interests should receive preferential treatment; others, useless or harmful to humans, might be neglected or extirpated. If we adopt this view, we should remember that organisms that do not directly contribute to human welfare are often necessary for the ecological health of the biotic community in which useful species thrive; as, for example, mycorrhizal fungi, that envelop the finer roots of forest trees and help them absorb nutrients from the soil, are of no direct use to people but contribute to the maintenance of forests where timber trees thrive. Moreover, we should not forget that nature is rich in aesthetic and intellectual as well as economic values, which unfortunately sometimes conflict. A land that yields a maximum of food, fibers, and other salable products might become so monotonous and uninteresting, so poor in aesthetic appeal, that our spirits might droop while we contemplate it. Narrow concentration on the welfare of humankind might in the long run be injurious to humans.

The task of preserving the natural world from destructive exploitation by an ever-growing mass of humans is so vast and many-sided that no individual, and probably no private organization or governmental agency, can effectively undertake all of it. Efficiency is promoted by specialization. It is fortunate that certain individuals or societies devote their efforts to protecting a small part of the natural community—rain forests, wetlands, dolphins, pandas, or whatever—without, I hope, forgetting that their specialty is only part of a much greater endeavor, that of saving the planet from utter spoliation; for unless we preserve the whole in a flourishing state, we cannot save the parts.

As an approach to conservation less daunting than biodiversity of indefinite compass, I suggest that we devote our efforts to biocompatibility, or compatible biodiversity, the harmonious association of diverse species. To start a program for biocompatibility, we should choose a large community of diverse creatures that coexist without destructive strife, or better, with mutual support, and then add whatever other organisms might be compatible with this nuclear group. An appropriate association is that of flowering plants, their pollinators, and the dispersers of their seeds. Such a community of reciprocally helpful plants and animals includes plants of many families and growth forms, from herbs and vines to towering trees; among their pollinators are bees, butterflies, moths, beetles, dipterous flies, and (in the New World) hummingbirds and certain tanagers; the disseminators of their seeds are a multitude of frugivorous birds, bats, and flightless mammals, including the widespread, terrestrial agoutis of tropical America. The plants attract the pollinators by their colors and fragrance, and reward them with nectar and excess pollen. With eagerly sought fruits and arillate seeds, they recompense the animals that digest only the soft pulp and spread viable seeds far and wide.

To injure the organism with which it exchanges benefits would not advantage any member of this association; only exceptionally do some break the unwritten "contract" by stealing nectar from flowers without pollinating them, as hummingbirds and bees occasionally do. Frugivorous birds rarely harm one another; the only exceptions to this rule in tropical American forests known to me are the great-billed toucans, who swallow fruits and disseminate seeds too big for the smaller birds in this guild, but they too often plunder the nests of lesser birds. Bees occasionally raid neighboring hives of different species, stubbornly fighting the residents and, if victorious, carrying off their stores of nectar and pollen. Like most things in this perplexing world, the plant-pollinator-disperser association is not perfect, but it is nevertheless one of evolution's most admirable achievements, contributing immensely to nature's harmony and productivity, and, especially by flowers, birds, and butterflies, to its beauty. Moreover, directly or indirectly, the association provides nourishment for a large proportion of terrestrial life.

To learn how many species belong to the plant-pollinator-disperser association in any given area might require a prolonged study by a team of botanists, entomologists, ornithologists, and mammalogists, which to my knowledge has never anywhere been made. I surmise that in a tract of temperate zone woodland the association would include hundreds of species. In a similar area of tropical rain forest, where wind pollination is much rarer than in the temperate zones and more winged pollinators are needed, the number might run into thousands. Around this nucleus cluster other species that are neither pollinators nor dispersers. Among them are many insectivorous birds and other creatures that coexist harmoniously with the dispersers, and are indeed indispensable to them, for without the former, insects might devour all the foliage and kill the plants that yield the fruits and nectar.

Less closely allied to the plant-pollinator-disperser association, but living harmoniously with it, are many other animals; in tropical American forests, tinamous, guans, quails, pigeons, and, among raptors, the Laughing Falcon, that subsists almost wholly upon snakes. Parrots that digest seeds instead of the pulp that surrounds them may slightly reduce the reproduction of trees but neither injure them nor harm other birds. Among mammals, armadillos, anteaters, sloths, many primates, and others also belong to the compatible community. Not to be excluded are the indispensable but more obscure multitudes of small organisms that decompose dead tissues or otherwise contribute to the soil's ability to support the association, greatly swelling its numbers.

Similar biocompatible associations are found in wetlands, prairies, Arctic tundra, and the oceans but apparently have not been investigated from this point of view. They appear to include fewer collaborators than those of woodlands. In the oceans, where the biomass of animals is very much greater in proportion to that of the chlorophyll-bearing plants that support them, the struggle for survival is fiercer and predation more rife, a truth to which the huge production of eggs of many marine creatures, far exceeding that of any terrestrial animals except possibly queen termites and bees, bears unimpeachable testimony. Nevertheless, in the oceans biocompatible associations do occur, as with cleaner fishes and their clients.

Preferential treatment of biocompatible associates would benefit the indispensable sustainers of terrestrial life but certainly not everything. It would protect neither invertebrate parasites nor parasitic cuckoos and cowbirds, all of which are only a froth (although often a smothering froth) on the surface of the living world. Whenever they seriously threaten human life or economic interests, vigorous, often costly efforts are made to exterminate them. Predatory vertebrates, especially among mammals and birds, present special problems. Mostly solitary, unsocial creatures, they do not fit into any biocompatible association, but on the contrary prey, often heavily, upon the members of such associations. Because many of them are big and powerful, they frequently excite humans' misplaced adulation of bigness and power (a major cause of their misfortunes), and not a few win admiration by their grace or beauty. Contributing little or nothing to the support of the living community (except its scavengers), they make heavy demands upon it. If not deliberately trying to reduce their numbers, a conservation program committed to biocompatibility rather than undefined biodiversity should at least stop spending all the money and effort now given to their protection and increase.

One of the gravest mistakes of wildlife management in our time is the reintroduction of predatory birds and mammals into areas where they have long been absent, such as the artificial establishment of Peregrine Falcons in cities. The undesirable, often disastrous, effects of introducing alien animals, even some admirable in themselves, into countries like Australia, New Zealand, and the United States have long been recognized and deplored. Reintroduction of large and dangerous species may become equally deplorable.

Predation is widely viewed as indispensable to prevent populations of animals becoming so numerous that they destroy their habitats, "eating themselves out of house and home." Even those who condemn predation as a major evil, a lamentable miscarriage of evolution, may grudgingly concede that it is a necessary evil. Nevertheless, the role of predation in regulating animal populations has been exaggerated. It is most obviously necessary in the case of large browsing and grazing quadrupeds-deer, antelopes, horned ruminants, elephants, and the like—which may so severely overexploit light woodland or grassland that it may take years to recover after the exploiters' numbers are reduced by widespread starvation. Where elephants are protected, they become too numerous and so damage their range that, despite sentiment, their herds must be culled to avert disaster. Shooting of excess individuals by expert marksmen is kinder than the methods of predators, which too often tear the flesh of still living victims.

When we turn to frugivorous and insectivorous birds, we find a very different situation. It is hardly an exaggeration to say that they are incapable of ruining their habitats. In an unfavorable season, fruits may become so scarce that hungry birds are reduced to eating them before they ripen, when they are harder to digest and less nourishing but may already contain viable seeds. The birds' reproduction may be depressed, and some may starve; but the fruit-bearing trees and shrubs will not be injured by premature removal of their fruits, and next year they can yield abundantly. Similarly, nectar drinkers can hardly injure flowering plants, even if, as sometimes happens, they damage flowers by piercing or tearing corollas to reach the sweet fluid. When nectar is scarce, they may turn to insects, as hummingbirds frequently do. Insectivorous birds can rarely glean so effectively that they exterminate the insects, spiders, and other small invertebrates that nourish them. With their rapid reproduction and reduced pressure upon them, they soon restore their populations and continue to support the insectivores.

Birds can regulate their populations without outside intervention. A widespread method is territoriality, which adjusts the number of breeding pairs to the areas and resources adequate for rearing their broods. The size of broods is correlated with the longevity of adults. At latitudes where the rigors of winter or the hazards of long migrations to escape winter reduce life expectancy, broods are substantially larger than are those of related species at low latitudes, where the average life span of resident birds is considerably longer. In contrast to mammals, which often begin to reproduce before they cease growing, many birds delay breeding for one or more years after they are full-grown. Extreme examples of this are long-lived marine birds, many of which do not breed until they are five to ten years old, and they lay only one egg, as among albatrosses.

"Pest birds," like Red-billed Queleas in Africa and Eared Doves in Argentina, appear to contradict the foregoing statements by building up excessive populations that devour field crops, especially grains. They live in artificial situations. Farmers unintentionally help them multiply, then complain when the birds take advantage of agricultural bounty. Predators fail to reduce the teeming populations of these birds enough to save the crops. Thus, we might say, with reference to birds, that predators are either unnecessary to control populations or are ineffective. The same appears to be true of many other kinds of animals, but to discuss this matter here would lead us too far astray.

As the forces of destruction increase and their weapons become more devastating, conservationists wage a losing war. It is time to reconsider our strategy. The promotion of biodiversity is unselective, supporting both our allies and our enemies in our major endeavor, which is to preserve ecosystems. When we analyze an ecosystem, we find it an association of organisms that by their diverse roles mutually support one another, as in the plant-pollinator-disperser alliance—thereby making and preserving the system, with a large admixture of organisms hostile to these key members of the system. The former support our efforts to preserve forests and other ecosystems, the latter oppose our efforts. Instead of maintaining an essentially neutral attitude toward the protagonists in the internal struggle that afflicts an ecosystem, we should throw our weight on the side of the defenders, giving them preferential treatment and whatever aid we can, perhaps not trying to exterminate all their enemies—in any case an impossible task—but at least not supporting them. If we humans could make ourselves more compatible with the biocompatible associations that are the mainstay of the natural world, we would form an alliance that might preserve it indefinitely.

After this digression, which seemed necessary to counter certain objections to a conservation program that would exclude from protection some of the most predatory vertebrates, let us return to the advantages of biocompatibility over unlimited biodiversity. In the first place, it would help to preserve the maximum sustainable number of individuals (our second alternative) of the protected, nonpredatory, or mildly predatory species, which are nearly always more numerous than the animals that prey upon them. In particular, it would help to retard the widely lamented decline of many species of birds, especially the Neotropical migrants. Predation is only one of several factors in their plight, but it is by no means negligible; raptors take a heavy toll of migrants, especially while they are concentrated at the staging places where they interrupt their journeys to replenish their depleted reserves of energy.

By benefiting the extremely important plant-pollinator-disperser association and its allies, biocompatibility would promote human economic interests (our third alternative). It would make close association with nature more rewarding and pleasant to the growing number of people who enjoy the majesty of trees and the beauty of flowers and birds and are distressed or repelled by the sight of predators striking down and tearing their victims and the hideously mangled remains of what yesterday was a beautiful animal going peaceably about its business and enjoying its life. By no conceivable effort could conservationists, however numerous and well funded they become, bring perfect harmony into the living world, but by their united efforts they might bring it a little closer to the realization of this ancient, widespread, and perennially attractive ideal.

The Troubled Childhood of Intelligence

The mind that can reason, understand, foresee, create, respond to beauty, feel sympathy and compassion, distinguish right from wrong, and remain ever sensitive to conscience is often, and doubtless rightly, regarded as the highest product of evolution on this planet. Only humans have such a mind in a more than rudimentary state, and we have it because, in the first place, we needed a big brain to guide the versatile hands that our earliest terrestrial progenitors inherited from ancestors whose forelimbs had been modified for climbing in trees and plucking fruits. Since foreseeing guidance is what the living world most lacked, we might suppose that such a mind would, from the beginning, exercise a consistently beneficent influence, and in the measure that it developed, might become an ever more powerful agent for creating high values, promoting harmony and happiness.

Alas!—the contrary is all too true. Although dawning intelligence soon gave humans great advantage over competing animals, it involved us in all sorts of difficulties. Confused and misused, it intensified strife, too frequently brought sorrow when it might have increased joy, and threatened to wreck the living world—a threat that today we feel more keenly than ever before. Why something with such great capacity for promoting all that is good has been the cause of so much evil is a paradox that we must now try to explain. Since intelligence supervened upon instinct, we must begin our inquiry with a glance at this large topic.

Instinct, Forerunner of Intelligence

We can hardly doubt that the activities of our remote ancestors were controlled largely by instincts, as, in varying degrees, is true of all other vertebrate animals, from fish and amphibians to birds and mammals. *Instinct* is one of those unfortunate words so often loosely used that we would like to avoid it, but we can hardly do so without using clumsy circumlocutions.

Of the subjective aspects of instinctive activities, we can only surmise. We cannot be certain whether an animal foresees the end of an instinctive performance or approaches it blindly. Nevertheless, one that demonstrates its ability to learn many things about its surroundings seems capable also of learning, from past performances of an innate series of actions, to expect a certain outcome. Moreover, if the structure of its brain and nervous system prepared it to accomplish, without instruction, some complicated task, such as the construction of a nest, it does not appear impossible for this same structure to create, in advance of all experience, a mental picture of the result.

This subjective aspect of the instinct might well be promoted by natural selection, for to have an image of the goal should help the animal to achieve it in variable circumstances. The fact that animals sometimes persist stubbornly in some instinctive activity in circumstances that preclude its successful termination is certainly not proof that they are not aware of what they are trying to do; for we, who pride ourselves that we know what we are about, occasionally exhibit similar stupidity. May not the human mind's lack of clear innate ideas result from the decay of those complex patterns of innate behavior that we call instincts?

Although the psychic aspect of instinctive behavior stirs the imagination of the sympathetic observer of animals, let us say no more about this fascinating subject and proceed to the more soluble problem of distinguishing instinctive activity from reflex action, on the one hand, and intelligent behavior, on the other, for between these two territories lies the half-explored realm of instinct. Instinctive activity differs from reflex action chiefly by its higher level of integration, so that between the two no precise boundary can be drawn. From a simple reflex, like scratching an irritating spot on the skin or blinking the eyes, an instinctive activity, such as building a nest by birds or wasps, differs, among other things, in the greater number of muscles involved, their more complex interactions, and the continuance of the activity over a longer interval, so that the integration is both spatial and temporal.

From intelligent behavior, instinctive behavior differs in that it is neither learned by the individual nor, in its main features, much improved by learning. Nevertheless, like other structures and functions, it is strengthened and perfected as the animal matures; and the fact that the animal may attempt clumsily to perform some instinctive activity before maturation is complete may give the impression that competence in its execution depends upon learning. Yet these first tentative efforts, these preliminary interactions with the environment that in many cases seem necessary to perfect the instinct, are perhaps not to be sharply distinguished from learning in the ordinary sense of the word.

Accordingly, we must recognize, as Hebb (1953) pointed out, that the special effect of environmental stimulation that we call learning plays an essential part in perfecting all so-called innate activities; just as learning itself would be impossible without a large endowment of innate capacities. All behavior, both instinctive and acquired, is dependent upon both heredity and the environment; in the former, the individual's experience is supplementary to the hereditary endowment, whereas in learned behavior the innate endowment is overshadowed by the individual's experience. The difference between instinctive and learned activities reduces itself, in the final analysis, to the relative weight of these two factors that jointly determine all behavior. In the absence of either, animal activity is hardly possible.

That instinctive behavior is adaptive or adjusted to promote the welfare of the individual and the perpetuation of its species is a conclusion that follows from prevailing views on the origin and mode of transmission of instincts. Since they are held to grow and change by successive genetic mutations, and are transmitted through the germ plasm rather than passed by example or instruction from generation to generation, only instincts beneficial to the species are likely to arise and to escape elimination by natural selection.

In conclusion, we might say that an instinctive activity consists of a series of coordinated acts into which an animal enters as a whole; it is transmitted genetically rather than by example or instruction; and it conforms rather closely to a pattern common to a whole population of animals and is, as a rule, essential to their continued prosperity.

THE TWO PHASES OF INSTINCTIVE BEHAVIOR

Instinctive activity is set in motion by some impulse, tension, or drive, which may be wholly internal or spontaneous in origin or may be awakened or strengthened by external stimuli acting upon an innate foundation or propensity. However initiated, the whole activity of an animal that in general follows innate patterns may conveniently be divided into two stages or phases, the appetitive and the consummatory. In the second phase, the animal completes some act of value to itself or its species, such as seizing and swallowing food, making a nest or shelter, performing stereotyped courtship rites, or sexual union with its mate. These consummatory acts are, as a rule, carried out in rather definite circumstances, with a sequence of movements that permits slight variation. The animal's whole organization, bodily and psychic, is set to perform these acts in a predetermined way.

But before an animal can seize and swallow food, it must find or overtake it; before it can dig a burrow or build a nest, it must choose a suitable site or select proper materials from the great variety that the locality may afford; before it can court a mate, it must find one.

In these and similar cases, the seeking and acquiring of the appropriate object or situation is known as appetitive behavior. This questing and selecting amid the endlessly variable conditions of the external world, with all its surprises and perils, demands greater plasticity that the consummatory act, which, rigid as it is, cannot be successfully performed until, from all possible conditions, the animal has placed itself in precisely those appropriate for the final stereotyped performance. Accordingly, it is the appetitive phase of behavior that chiefly demands keen senses, awareness of ends, ability to adjust swiftly to sudden changes in circumstances, judgment—in brief, intelligence and the ability to learn by experience.

It is significant that in the growing animal the consummatory phase of instinctive activity often appears before the appetitive phase. One sees young birds going through the movements of picking up inedible objects before they have searched for and found proper food, of digging a burrow before they have found an earthen bank, of building a nest before they have selected a site or gathered materials. These stereotyped procedures, for which nerves and muscles are already set, may thus be carried out as though in a vacuum, without reference to appropriate external conditions or their place in the whole pattern of the animal's life. In the more mature animal, going about the proper business of its kind, the appetitive phase necessarily precedes the consummatory phase: it must find food before it eats, select a site before it builds its nest. The student of animal behavior, trying to discover how much his subjects can learn, or what intelligence they display in solving problems and overcoming difficulties, is significantly concerned with the appetitive phase of behavior, which is where intelligence first appears in the living world. In these tests, food is usually the incentive, or else escape from an uncomfortable situation. The animal is required to pit its wits against the variable circumstances of the external world that threaten to overcome it, or to surmount obstacles interposed between itself and the satisfaction of its appetite.

We can hardly overestimate the full significance of the place and manner in which intelligence was inserted into the system of animal behavior, and the profound influence this was to exert on the subsequent history of mind. It was not in the performance of highly integrative, constructive activities that intelligence first acquired value. The whole immensely complex business of organic growth, the coordination of the body's manifold functions, recuperation from the effects of strenuous activity—all these had long been accomplished without conscious guidance. Likewise, such constructive occupations as building a nest, winning a mate, and caring for young, could follow stereotyped hereditary patterns, owing nothing to deliberate planning or forethought, whenever the proper or normal conditions were present. It was to deal with the variable and frequently hostile circumstances of the external world that intelligence was born. To capture prey, to outwit predators, to defeat competitors for a mate or homesite, to overcome the difficulties and obstructions of the endlessly mutable environment— such endeavors demanded a flexibility of behavior scarcely compatible with fixed inborn patterns.

In the performance of stereotyped consummatory acts an animal is like a machine all primed and set, needing only the touch of a button to release a train of movements that will automatically continue until the task is done. But appetitive behavior, often carried on under stress and making great demands upon the animal's persistence and endurance, might relax and prematurely cease without strong and persistent motivation. Appropriate appetites and emotions were needed to keep the animal eager and tense for the sustained effort. And what affective states would fittingly accompany endeavors such as we have specified? Hunger as a nagging discomfort to goad it to find food; fierceness to steel it to spring upon its prey; fear of its pursuer to spur it onward to the last gasp of breath; hatred of rivals; rage when thwarted; enmity toward all that frustrated and opposed it. Thus, neither the activities that dawning intelligence directed, nor the emotions that incited and accompanied them, were concordant with the central character and primary determinant of life, which, as we have seen, is essentially an integrative, constructive process, expressing itself in friendly, cooperative attitudes. Intelligence was enlisted as an auxiliary skirmisher to confront threats to life's peaceful advance.

THE TRANSFER FROM INSTINCTIVE TO INTELLIGENT GUIDANCE

Even in the more intelligent of contemporary animals, intelligence appears at best to play a minor role. In complex innate patterns of behavior, the main features of which are little subject to modification by reason or learning, it intervenes chiefly at the more flexible articulations, where freedom to adjust to variable circumstances is of greatest value. To advance much beyond this point, intelligence needs a number of special conditions, which are found in humans alone.

In the first place, intelligence requires organs to make its insights effective. Hoofed animals appreciate protection from rain; but if it ever occurred to a horse or a cow to build of poles and leaves a simple thatched shelter, such as a human with primitive tools can make, their limbs are useless for such operations. Second, because the number of fresh insights that come to an individual in the course of its life is likely to be small, and the amount of information it can accumulate by its own unaided efforts rather limited, some means of transmitting such acquisitions is of the greatest importance. Although the example of elders may help the young animal to learn, speech is the most effective means of conveying information. Finally, only the decay of compelling innate patterns of behavior can make an animal free to introduce innovations into its lifestyle. The loss of these genetically transmitted patterns would leave the animal without vital guidance if its opportunities to learn from others of its kind did not simultaneously increase. Only in a social animal with adequate means of communication are the conditions for any considerable growth of intelligence realized.

It would be wrong to leave the impression that intelligence could ever supplant the whole innate equipment signified by the term *instinct* in its broadest sense. This includes those motives, drives, or internal tensions that, with or without external stimulation, set the animal in motion. In general, while weak these impulses or internal stresses require some stimulus or enticement from outside to release the appropriate activity, but when strong enough they

may start a train of movements in the absence of external exci-
tations and even of the conditions necessary for their fruitful performance. In animals with a full complement of instincts, these
appetites and drives initiate behavior that flows through definitely
channeled courses. Of these innate patterns, we retain only remnants, insufficient to guide us through life. Some students of
human behavior regard sleeping as an instinct; and since without
instruction babies can learn to walk, this might also be classified as
an instinctive activity, like crying, sucking, and grasping some support to avoid falling, although these seem to be hardly more than
reflex acts.

Compared to the breadth and richness of detail of those beautiful, full-flowered innate patterns that guide a bird in winning a mate,
building a nest, and rearing its young, surviving human instincts are
at best poor remnants. But if we have lost nearly all the innate
equipment that steers an animal through its varied activities, we
retain without much impairment the appetites, impulses, and drives
that demand satisfaction. Indeed, we have acquired many new
incentives to action. Since intelligence is a guide and never a motive
power, without these innate, nonrational appetites and drives the
most rational animal might never take a step, think a thought, or
speak a word, for it would lack the vital impulse to act. Even our
most abstract intellectual activities are instigated by special impulses
or appetites, often springing from those depths of our being to
which conscious intelligence can scarcely penetrate.

The growth of intelligence, then, is the process of replacing
innate patterns of behavior by another guide, while retaining some
or all of those inborn appetites and drives that impel animals to
act. Meanwhile, the lineage of animals in which this transfer is
slowly effected must continue uninterruptedly to run life's perilous
race, for to pause is to perish. This change of command is obviously a hazardous procedure, like changing generals in the midst
of a battle, or jumping from one horse to another while galloping
at full speed. Begun many thousands if not millions of years ago in
our ancestors, who were doubtless still more apelike than human,
the transfer is today still far from complete. Unless we remember

that the whole story of humankind, including the most recent history, covers a difficult period of readjustment, of transition from one mode of control or integration of activities to another quite different, we shall not read this story with understanding, and contemplation of the human drama, with its innumerable follies and consequent miseries, may fill us with loathing and despair, unlighted by a ray of hope.

THE GIGANTIC TASK OF NASCENT INTELLIGENCE

Intelligence is, above all, the ability to link ideas, and the movements they guide, in new combinations. An ape, inspired by a flash of insight, as in W. Köhler's (1927) experiments, seizes a stick and knocks down a tempting fruit that hangs above his reach. Undoubtedly he was already somewhat familiar with sticks and their properties, with fruits, and with falling bodies, and now he has combined these elements of his experience in a novel way that leads to the desired result. Let us not lose sight of the fact that this association was not possible without dissociation. If the animal and all his ancestors have instinctively climbed to reach or shake down fruit, his fresh insight will bring him no advantage unless he can break the established sequence in which sight of an edible fruit hanging overhead is followed by climbing instead of by picking up a stick. Obviously, such ability to disrupt or dissolve patterns of behavior that for generations have adequately guided one's kind is fraught with insidious dangers. But the free association of ideas is such a perilous adventure that we must give it greater attention.

Those who have studied science or philosophy, or grown up among people of good practical intelligence, have learned to associate ideas in so many profitable combinations that they seldom stop to consider that these represent only a fraction of the possible ways of associating the same elements of experience. How bewildered we would be if all our articulated series of ideas were to fly asunder, and we were confronted with the task of arranging the loose components into coherent, practically useful patterns without benefit of the accumulated experience of men and women! Of the many principles or schemas by which the simplest facts or ideas can be associated, some are worthless, if not positively misleading. Science is cultivated by people with trained minds, yet one who traces its history sometimes suspects that not until all possible false theories have been tried and found inadequate can the most fruitful explanation of each natural phenomenon win acceptance. The construction of a sound theory depends upon combining the pertinent facts in an order that reflects the structure of nature rather than some idiosyncracy of the investigator's mind.

If scientists and philosophers so frequently blunder in this way, how must it have been with our remote ancestors, whose dawning intelligence confronted a bewildering array of experiences that cried insistently for explanation but who had not yet developed the most elementary canons of reason or of scientific investigation? Only by a stupendous process of trial and error could the profitable combinations of ideas be discovered and the vastly greater number of worthless ones rejected. The pains, the heartaches, the frustrations, the waste of time and energy, and blood and life exacted by this process are the price humankind had perforce to pay for abandoning well-tried instinctive patterns of behavior for the perilous privilege of experimenting with novel combinations of the elements of thought and action. The search for sound, enduring arrangements of these elements continues unabated to the present day. We are still far from having the ideally best pattern of human life; but when we recall how much of the preliminary exploration was done for us by our rude, blundering, unlettered ancestors of long ago, we shall join Sir James Frazer (1922) in acknowledging our debt to the savage.

TRAGIC CONSEQUENCES OF FREE MENTAL ACTIVITY

The only associations of ideas of practical value are those that reflect the structure of reality. All others are not only worthless but misleading, a perpetual liability to people who entertain them. The associations of greatest practical value are those that express cause and effect and inherence and subsistence. By the first, we predict consequences by their antecedents; by the second, we recognize objects by their qualities. In either case, the constancy of the relationship is our only warrant of its soundness. If, when we see smoke, we can always trace it to a fire, we are justified in concluding that fire is the cause of smoke. If a globular, orange object with a certain peculiar texture and aroma always proves, on closer scrutiny, to be an orange, we take these properties to be adequate signs of an edible fruit.

In addition to these and a few other profitable modes of association, there are many more, equally or perhaps more congenial to the human mind, that only prolonged and often unhappy experience can expose as the specious delusions they are. Thus, we naturally associate any detached part with the whole from which it came. This is especially true of organic bodies; so that we readily associate hair or nail parings, or any excretion, or even any discarded particle of food or scrap of clothing that has been in intimate contact with a human body, with the body itself. And it is common experience that a slight alteration of a small part of a living body may produce profound changes in the whole, as when a scratch on a finger leads to an infection that may be fatal. What could be more obvious to naive intelligence than that appropriate treatment of such detached trifles cannot fail to affect the person so indissolubly connected with them in thought? In the long, dim centuries of the past, and continuing today among traditional peoples, an unbelievable amount of human energy has gone into the spells and magic rites applied to such morsels in the belief that the erstwhile owner would thereby come to some harm, perhaps sicken and die; and people who have known or even suspected that shorn locks of their hair, parings of their fingernails, or discarded scraps of their food have fallen into an enemy's hands have suffered agonies of apprehension that sometimes led to their death. Such tremendous waste and misery have resulted from the apparently trivial error of confusing a mental association with an organic connection!

Or consider the errors arising from false analogies. It is obvious that when one animal eats another, something, which today we call matter or energy, passes from the victim's body to that of its devourer. Is it so illogical to suppose that other properties of the victim—its courage, cunning, fleetness, or strength—should be transmitted with its flesh in similar fashion; so that by eating a lion's heart one might acquire boldness; from an antelope, fleetness; from a hare, timidity; from a brave man, courage; and perhaps even wisdom from a sage? Countless victims, human no less than animal, have had their throats cut or their hearts torn out as an oblation to this mistaken notion; while other creatures, possessed of qualities less admired, have in consequence of this same error been spared the fate to which their palatable flesh might otherwise have consigned them.

A false analogy fraught with more tragic consequences was that between a human kingdom and the world. Until recently, many a kingdom was governed by an autocrat who carried out his will by means of edicts, was terrible to his subjects when thwarted, but could be placated by gifts, supplications, or displays of groveling humility. The whole visible world, with all the invisible spirits supposed to dwell therein, often seemed to immature intelligence to be just such a kingdom on a vaster scale, ruled by an even more powerful monarch who remained unseen, accomplished his purposes by fiats, and prostrated his subjects by plague, earthquake, flood, or famine when incensed with them but who could be appeased by gifts, supplications, and expiatory rites. How many victims have groaned, how many altars have reeked with flesh and blood of man and beast alike, in consequence of this mistaken but not unnatural analogy!

It is needless to multiply examples. Works on anthropology and even history abound with them, and similar "vulgar errors" continue to lurk among the less educated inhabitants of enlightened modern nations. Here it will suffice to point out that confusion so innocent in intention, but often so terrible in its consequences, is the natural, inevitable result of the mind's newly acquired capacity to associate its thoughts in fresh combinations, the value of which can be tested only in the hard school of experience. Like many another novelty, free intelligence entered the world bringing confusion and discord in its train, and a long process of harmonization, still far from completion, was needed to undo the harm wrought, heal the lesions it caused, and combine the new with the old in a higher, ampler synthesis.

The human mind liberated itself from the benevolent despotism of fixed patterns of behavior only to fall into the destructive anarchy of false and too often mischievous notions. Thus began the turbulent era of the growing pains of intelligence, which has continued uninterrupted for certainly no less than fifty thousand years, and possibly a good many millenia more. If their cranial capacity may be taken as an index, people of late Paleolithic times had minds capable of forming as many, or almost as many, connections between ideas as ours can. The ways in which the raw elements of experience could be grouped were many. These associations might arise as a result of casual juxtapositions of events in space or time, or of superficial resemblances, or of fortuitous similarities between words. Accidental connections between ideas led to innumerable false conclusions—too many to be corrected in the lifetime of one individual, even a thinker as capacious and indefatigable as Aristotle himself. The errors made by prehistoric people do not prove that their innate mental ability was less than ours, for the best contemporary minds might fall into them without the guidance of the past, transmitted by the written and spoken word. A large part of the tedious process of reaching truth consists in breaking wrong connections between ideas, perpetuated by the society in which we live, while sound connections are strengthened and disseminated. As we accomplish this gigantic task, intelligence comes of age. To complete the work, the cumulative efforts of many generations of thinkers are needed. Yet the quest of truth can never stop; in a developing world, it is endless.

THE CURSE OF CURIOSITY

A natural outgrowth of the ability to associate ideas in patterns not controlled by heredity or concrete experience is curiosity. As presented to us by the external world, events occur in finite series which are causal or relational, and the middle terms of such series are joined on both sides to others. But the extreme members of these series lack an associate on the outer side. They seem to stand with one hand gripping a companion and the other groping blindly in the void, feeling for a friendly hand-clasp. Beyond the last object visible on the horizon must be something else that vision fails to reveal. Beyond the smallest visible particle must be others too minute to discern. Beyond the earliest event recorded in history were others of which history is silent. Beyond the latest incident in our lives looms the future, necessary to complete the series but exasperatingly hidden from us. Curiosity is the effort to extend the nexus of relations that experience reveals to us beyond the limits that confine experience in every direction, to proceed from the immediately given to the logically necessary.

A mind in which the combinations of ideas are wholly controlled by experience rests placidly within the limits of the given, content with what immediately occupies it and unconcerned about all else. It is not likely to be perturbed by fear of the unseen, by apprehension of the future, or by questions about the unexperienced past. But an intelligence that can associate ideas freely is forever restlessly sniffing about, like a dog that has lost its master in a crowd. In children this inner necessity to extend the series of ideas beyond immediate experience leads to the questioning age, when adults are harassed by incessant queries. In the long history of our species, a corresponding stage probably supervened upon a period when hominids accepted facts as they were given, like infants and domestic animals; and with no wise parent or elder sibling to provide correct answers to the innumerable questions that humans of the dawn were beginning to ask, confusion was bound to result. As Bühler (1930) suggested, if humankind ever enjoyed a time of paradisiacal clarity and innocence, it was due to the absence of that restless and boring "Why?"

Although the astronomer is curious about the remotest stars and the historian about the most distant past, the curiosity of most people is stirred chiefly by what will happen to them in the future, and why they suffer, as from accident, disease, or thwarted hope. So insistent is the need to extend the sequence of ideas in these directions that people will have answers at any price and will stop at no absurdity if only their curiosity may be satisfied. And there was never a lack of clever people ready to exploit neighbors who combined imperious curiosity with boundless credulity, who needed desperately to know why a loved member of the family was sick, why a plague or a famine afflicted a city, or how a war or some other hazardous enterprise would succeed. Hence arose multitudes of prophets, augurs, diviners, astrologers, necromancers, oneirocritics, and all the countless varieties of soothsayers and fortune-tellers. Hence oracles, with their ecstatic pythonesses and rich treasuries, like those at Delphi and Dodona, dotted the ancient lands. Many a victim poured out its innocent blood and had its bowels torn open so that the portents might be read in its entrails; many a distracted father, husband, or ruler was persuaded to do penance, to sacrifice cherished possessions, or even children, so that the angry gods might be appeased and stop the plague, cease to withhold the rain, or cause the wind to blow, as when Iphigenia was immolated at Aulis. Curiosity is the precursor of science and the array of useful inventions that it gives us; but since the first curious ape rudely tore apart some unoffending flower or insect, how many ills that mentally placid animals avoid has it brought upon primate animals and the unfortunate creatures that fall into their clutches!

THE FALSIFICATION OF VALUES

Closely associated with the confusion of thought that fell upon dawning intelligence was the falsification of values, especially in the field of aesthetics. The subject is difficult because judgments of beauty differ so widely. That in which one person delights as beautiful another deems ugly, and who shall arbitrate between them? The only objective standards of beauty seem to be harmony among the distinguishable parts of an object or scene, faithfulness to nature, conformity to the spontaneous rhythms of the human mind and body, or congruence with the enduring purposes of life. Only by looking to nature for our criteria of beauty can we confidently assert that tribal forms of body decoration—alarming in our eyes—are expressions of an erring, unformed, or vitiated taste. We may wonder how it could ever have occurred to anybody that man or woman is improved or made more comely by such practices, widespread among traditional peoples and not absent among those of more advanced cultures, as flattening or otherwise deforming the skull by binding in infancy, scarifying the face and body, enlarging lips or ear-lobes to monstrous size, perforating the lips and nasal septum, dwarfing the feet, cultivating steatopygy, and similar distortions of the human form. Less startling, but equally expressive of a taste different from ours, are tattooing and loading the body with an excessive weight of jewelry and other adornments. The grotesque images of gods that certain peoples have worshipped may be the reflections of a fearsome theology, or they may spring from a grotesque aesthetic taste.

As people's thoughts become clearer, their artistic creations, as judged by the natural criteria that I have proposed, tend also to improve, although there are doubtless exceptions to this rule. One thinks of the Greeks, whose clear vision of nature and ideal of a balanced life guided by reason had as its counterpart in art the creation of forms so faithful to their originals that they still delight us. In Egypt, Ikhnaton's revolt against enthralling tradition and his simplification of religious thought went hand in hand with freer and more natural expression in art. The Italian renaissance was a movement of liberation in art no less than in thought, a turning to nature as the ultimate source of beauty no less than of truth. In all parts of the world, in the measure that humans have freed their minds of old errors and debasing superstitions, their art has become more faithful to natural models. One wonders whether some of the unusual turns that modern art has taken are not a manifestation of intellectual degeneration. The half-formed mind turns away from nature; the mature mind returns to it.

Some of the aesthetic values we may consider false, both in other cultures and in our own, appear to result from another derangement of value. So great has been the loss of vital integrity caused by confused thinking that people have tended to become incapable of evaluating any situation in their own lives on its own merits; they have become unduly concerned with how they would appear to others. When a person chooses a covering for the body, the chief consideration is not its comfort and suitability to the climate, but whether it enhances social prestige. The same motive makes him or her submit to the painful operations of cicatrizing, tattooing, or even deforming the body, sometimes ruining its natural grace. In marriage, too, love and the real worth of a nuptial partner have often been subordinated to the material, social, or political advantages of the alliance.

In countless instances, sound values have been compromised or sacrificed for the spurious values of external approval. Satisfactions have not been permitted to sprout at the points where they would spontaneously grow, but have again and again perversely been grafted upon some unnatural stock. Such subordination of vital to artificial values would not be so pathetic if it promoted happiness, but its effect is often just the reverse. Since the natural human being is often readier to find fault with than to praise neighbors, to sacrifice one's own satisfaction for the applause of others frequently brings joy to nobody. The very foundations of contentment are undermined by this perversion of values, which, springing from intellectual confusion, is one of the afflictions of intelligence in its formative stage.

THE RANK GROWTH OF SPECIAL MOTIVES

As though error, gullible curiosity, and the falsification of values, with all the consequent waste, pain, and confusion, has not sufficiently afflicted a humanity struggling to master the new gift of free intelligence, a possibly even worse calamity befell us in the guise of exaggerated special motives. When animal behavior is governed by innate patterns, each of its components is held within bounds by its place in the comprehensive system, which is organized into a hierarchy of ever wider scope, with the total welfare of the species at the top. The pleasure an animal may derive from eating, courting, drowsing in the sunshine, or some other occupation is rarely sufficiently alluring to foment the activity to the point where it upsets the creature's balance. One may devote years to observing free animals without witnessing gluttony, acquisitiveness, or sexual indulgence carried to the point where it diminishes the animal's fitness, involves it in recognized and avoidable perils, or incapacitates it for rearing its young. This vital sanity of nonhuman creatures was recognized by Plutarch in his unfinished dialogue, wherein Gryllus, transformed into a pig by Circe, tries to convince Ulysses that animals are superior to humans in temperance and fortitude. In so far as subjective states influence the animal's behavior, the happiness, satisfaction, or restful feeling that comes from maintaining all the components of its hereditary pattern of activities in due order and balance appears to be the compelling motive. From vital integrity as the dominant value in animal life, it is not difficult to trace the origin of conscience.

But, as we have learned, new associations could not be formed without dissolving old associations, free intelligence could not arise save as fixed patterns of behavior lost their compelling force. In this dissolution of hereditary patterns, the hierarchial order of activities was weakened, and now one special motive, now another, was free to take supreme, if temporary, command of the mind. And each appetite and passion, as it assumed paramount authority, had in its employ an ever more competent intelligence, which, like a conscienceless genie, was wholly at the disposal of its pleasure-loving master. We earlier noticed the points at which intelligence first intruded into the pattern of instinctive behavior and the tasks that chiefly devolved upon it. The deep, vital, constructive functions were much too intricate to be entrusted to a nascent intellect that could only now and then be aroused to activity and was fit only to guide appetitive behavior, in which it might help to surprise prey, outwit rivals, overcome obstacles, find shelter or a mate, or escape enemies. The passions associated with these pursuits were often greed, anger, hatred, rage, lust, and fear, to which were eventually added vanity, pride, and cruelty. Each of these explosive or disruptive affections might seize control of a half-formed but far from contemptible intelligence, like a hot-headed youth at the wheel of a powerful motorcar with a defective steering gear. To this alarming predicament had nascent intelligence brought humankind.

Had each individual been as independent and self-directed as many mammals and birds, humanity might never have weathered the tempests that the first crude stirrings of intelligence brewed in its bosom. As it happened, humans at this stage lived in closely knit groups founded upon blood relationship, and the family or clan would suffer from the individual's uncontrolled indulgence of appetite or passion. For its safety, each group tried to restrain the actions of its members. In traditional societies, direct injury to another individual is, as a rule, regarded as an offense against the aggrieved family rather than, as in more advanced cultures, against the State; and the injured person or his or her relatives are expected to settle accounts with the offender. But acts believed to jeopardize the whole tribe are treated in a quite different manner. Often they are regarded as affronts to the tribe's supernatural guardians, who will punish such insults in their own peculiar fashion, making the whole group suffer. These spirits so touchy and quick to take offence are perhaps hardly more than external projections of the inner disquietude that followed the disruption of the innate pattern of activities by nascent intelligence.

Thus arose mental attitudes that regarded with deepest abhorrence all those acts, often quite innocent in modern eyes, which might release malign influences upon the community. Such acts were inhibited by the taboo, infraction of which was more severely punished than was the mere murder of a fellow group member. Often the penalty was expulsion from the community, which to primitive people was almost equivalent to a death sentence. Nor was there a lack of other expedients for discouraging divergent conduct and enforcing conformity to tribal mores. In some tribes, including among the Bantu peoples of Africa, an outstanding innovation might be attributed to witchcraft and punished with the most fearful cruelty. This attitude discouraged progress as we now measure it; but perhaps, on the whole, the enforced external stagnation was beneficial rather than deplorable. Humans needed to grow inwardly, to come to terms with their dawning intelligence, before they were ready to embark upon a course of rapid changes in their lifestyles. We sometimes suspect that our contemporary world would be happier if the flood of innovations could somehow be retarded.

Despite taboos and punishments for witchcraft, tribal societies appear to have been less able to control self-willed, forceful individuals than modern states are. How precariously balanced is the character of people in the ruder stages of human development, how inadequate their inhibitions and superstitions for the control of conduct, is attested by the history of contacts between less and more advanced cultures. Whether the "savage" or "barbarian" meets "civilization" in the guise of conqueror, as did the Germanic hordes that overran the Roman Empire, or as the abject vanquished people, innumerable pathetic examples of which are provided by the annals of the expansion of Western Europe in the last four or five centuries, the result is typically the same: profound disorientation, greater readiness to adopt the vices than the virtues of the more advanced culture, sometimes relaxation of the will to live.

The severest test of a mature intellect and developed character is the ability to pursue a steadfast course amid all the world's fluctuating circumstances, to be immune alike to the numbing blasts of adversity and the flattering solicitations of prosperity, to preserve in solitude or amid the crowd the same principles of conduct. Whatever their level of material culture, people who have achieved this integrity are civilized in the best meaning of the word. On the whole, traditional peoples are too dependent upon their group for guidance and moral support to preserve such constancy of character when tribal bonds are loosened by foreign contacts. As though instinctively aware of this danger, some tribes resort to the most drastic means to avoid all intercourse with alien cultures. When he planned the model community described in the *Laws*, Plato recognized that such isolation contributes greatly to social and moral stability.

Barbaric Magnificence and Barbarous Ideals

The dawn of written history in southern Asia and around the eastern Mediterranean reveals peoples who in the arts and politics have passed beyond the earlier stages when people of approximately equal status lived in small groups ruled by tradition instead of a king. We behold a stratified society, in which the governing classes enjoyed great power and almost unlimited opportunities for the indulgence of their whims. Despite the glamor that auroral tints and the fancy of inspired bards have cast over this dawn of civilization, the pictures presented by the Homeric epics, by the Greek tragedies woven about half-mythical events already some centuries past, by the Egyptian and Assyrian inscriptions, by the historical passages of the Old Testament, or by the *Mahabharata* of ancient India—these pictures are profoundly disquieting. Whether we read of the rape of Helen, Achilles' wrath, Clytemnestra's vengeance, the unspeakable deeds of Pelop's line, the vainglory of the pharaohs, the Assyrian despots' craze for bloodshed, the good Yudhishthir's disastrous addiction to gambling, or the sinful concupiscence of worthy King David, we receive glimpses of a world in which the most memorable events were motivated by inordinate disruptive passions. If we suspect that the motives for some of the events reported in our oldest literary treasures were simplified or exaggerated for artistic purposes, it is only necessary to recall how much of the political history of later ages has been the result of similar passions.

We may wonder what kept these early societies going from generation to generation; why did they not consume themselves in the flames of their own excesses? Doubtless it was the common people, unconsidered and unsung, toiling stubbornly to fill the royal granaries and fashion the heroes' arms, pouring out their despised blood as footmen in the king's armies, who by their closeness to the soil, their steady adherence to ancestral ways, grimly carried on from century to century and restored all the destruction wrought by their too greedy, passionate, and ambitious rulers.

The barbaric splendor of the heroic age, the indulgence of pride, vainglory, and the craving for display by the ruling class on so vast a scale, was made possible by the advances in agriculture and practical arts accomplished by forgotten people of the Neolithic age. As Gordon Childe (1942) has pointed out, the new developments in agriculture, the domestication of animals, metallurgy, spinning and weaving, ceramics, building, and other techniques during the two millenia from about 6000 to 4000 B.C. effected an improvement in the material conditions of human life such as was hardly equaled by the whole long interval that separated this era from the beginning of the industrial revolution in the eighteenth century.

As to agriculture, no subsequent period can claim achievements equal to those of our prehistoric ancestors. If we regard world agriculture as a single great edifice, the foundations were laid and the walls raised to nearly their present height by illiterate souls who could not record their accomplishments in writing; and all that literate or civilized people have done throughout the whole historic period has been to add a few statues and diverse ornaments to the façade, and to devise more efficient means of keeping the building in repair, as by chemical fertilizers and the deliberate development of disease-resistant strains of economic plants. In the invention of improved machinery for sowing and harvesting, the application of mechanical power to agricultural operations, and the increase of yields per acre, much has been accomplished in the last two centuries; but the plants on which the modern world depends for food and clothing were nearly all discovered and domesticated by stone age ancestors, who also worked out the basic principles of caring for them.

The primary effect of the substitution of agriculture for primitive hunting and food gathering was to diminish the strife between humans and the animals on which they were accustomed to prey, and to enable more people to dwell peacefully together in a given area, where the production of food was vastly increased by the new art. But why, after the good start they had made before the dawn of history, did humans almost cease to advance the beneficent work? Why did agriculture, like other arts and crafts, stagnate or progress so slowly during so many centuries?

The answer appears to be that the first grand period of agricultural and technical progress created conditions that made further advances increasingly difficult. This happened because people were not yet ready to make good and constructive use of the leisure, the freedom from incessant preoccupation with filling the stomach, the ease and the power, that husbandry and the newly perfected crafts now gave them. The attention of many of the more able or aggressive men was diverted from the cultivation of the fields and the manufacture of useful wares to other more amusing but less constructive pursuits. Their minds were filled with vain thoughts and they ran after glittering baubles. Their consuming ambition was to display wealth and power, to impress their peers with the magnificence of their attire, the grandeur of their palaces, the multitude of their dependents and concubines and slaves, the breadth of their conquests, and the number of their victims. Those who were more astute and grasping wrung from the sweating husbandmen and artisans the surplus of their labor, permitting them to keep the bare pittance necessary to sustain life and continue their toil. These toilers, ground into the dust, had neither leisure nor incentive to advance the admirable work so well begun by ancestors who still lived in small communities of free and essentially equal people, cultivating their fields together.

Moreover, the frequent wars and conquests instigated by the thirst for power and military glory greatly increased the number of slaves, upon whom, in the richer lands, fell an ever-increasing share of agricultural and industrial production. The opulent class who enjoyed the leisure to observe, to speculate, or to experiment with new processes had also the power to command others to work for them, hence they had little incentive to develop tools and methods that eased the burden of the oppressed laborer. Then, too, they evidently lacked that minute familiarity with the methods of production that is indispensable for their improvement. Even worse, since a great part of the community's manual labor was performed by slaves or freedmen, to work with one's hands became a mark of social inferiority, beneath the dignity of a well-born citizen. Things came to such a pass that Aristotle could write that it was impossible for an artisan or slave to cultivate virtue—as he conceived it. The abundance of cheap or forced labor and disdain of manual operations perhaps explain why no ancient people, not even the Greeks with all their intellectual penetration and ingenuity, advanced far in the sciences that require experimentation and the construction of apparatus that is often elaborate, and why none invented much labor-saving machinery. It remained for a society that was outgrowing slavery and serfdom to progress notably in these fields.

It appears that the foundations of agriculture, and to a lesser extent of the crafts, were laid under the influence of deep vital urges impelling humanity toward ends it could not well foresee. Perhaps, if we could trace the origins of agriculture in detail, we would find that it began in much the same way as did the cultivation, by leaf-cutting Atta ants, of a special nutritious fungus on a carefully prepared medium; that it was essentially a biological development, owing much to mutation and selection, rather than a deliberate invention like the telephone or the airplane. One can readily understand why, in a later age, people in different lands attributed to gods or demigods the introduction of their cultivated plants, the domestication of fire, the arts of spinning and weaving, and other life-giving and life-preserving knowledge. But husbandry gave increased leisure to a privileged minority, whose still undisciplined minds spun all sorts of vain and mischievous notions. The deep, central impulses of humans as living beings were buried beneath superficial whims and fancies, which did not fail to be pernicious because they were shallow. Agriculture stagnated while empires expanded and cities grew more populous and corrupt.

The growth of civilization became a process wherein the two strata of society, the rulers and the toilers, mutually depraved each other. The laborers spoilt the rich by providing them with an excess of goods that permitted their indulgence in harmful luxuries and foolish ambitions. The rich ruined the poor by depriving them of the products of their toil, so that they could neither live decently nor cultivate their minds, nor preserve their self-respect. And humanity as a whole ceased to progress in the cultivation of harmony among people and with the rest of nature. In some ways, it fell below the level it had reached in Neolithic times, waging more destructive wars and more wantonly persecuting other animals.

Already some four thousand years ago, the craving for power, wealth, and luxury—and the social injustice and inequality resulting from that craving—brought on in Egypt an attitude of tedium and disgust that Breasted (1933) called "the earliest disillusionment." It had become evident that the chief obstacle to human welfare was not the hostility or parsimony of nature, nor yet the deficiency of human intelligence, but inability to free this intelligence from domination by those special appetites and passions in ministering to which it had so long been exercised and sharpened, so that it might be devoted unreservedly to the welfare of the whole person and of the great living community to which we belong. The two most pressing problems that we have faced are to control our environment and to control ourselves. It is in the second of these tasks that we have most conspicuously failed. To this failure we owe the greater part of our sorrows, and even a long interval of relative stagnation in our effort to make the best use of the resources that nature provides for us.

ABERRATIONS OF DAWNING INTELLIGENCE IN OTHER ANIMALS

We have no reason to suppose that some unfortunate quirk of the human mind is responsible for all the tragic misuses of its dawning intelligence that we have noticed. On the contrary, we have grounds for believing that such aberrations are inseparable from the growth of intelligence, and that any animal that developed intellectual capacity of the same order as that in humans would pass through a corresponding stage and exhibit its alarming symptoms.

Monkeys and apes are notoriously destructive. If the Chimpanzees studied by W. Köhler could lay hands on anything breakable, they could not rest until they had reduced it to parts that resisted further disintegration. However, he suggested that it was only the great apes' superior strength that enabled them to outdo human children in destructive analysis. These Chimpanzees delighted in thrusting a pointed stick against the legs or body of any unsuspecting person or animal that came near. They enticed chickens up to the bars of their enclosure by offering food, then, withdrawing the proferred morsel, they jabbed the poor birds with sticks or pieces of wire. They would also poke and tap a lizard, perhaps more out of curiosity and excitement than cruelty, until it succumbed. The misbehavior of Köhler's Chimpanzees might be attributed to the boredom of captivity; but the free Chimpanzees that Jane van Lawick-Goodall (1971) studied in Tanzania were hardly less destructive, breaking and tearing tents, furniture, clothing, and bedding. The cleverer of these apes learned to open all the fastenings that their human friends devised for the boxes that held coveted bananas. The captive white-faced Cebus Monkey that Thomas Belt (1888) kept in Nicaragua enticed ducklings within reach by displaying bread, then caught them and killed them by a bite in the breast. Similar behavior by humans at a certain stage of mental development is too well known to require comment.

It might be supposed that this similarity of the behavior of monkeys and apes to that of rude people and unguided children is merely an expression of tendencies widespread in primates but not shared by other branches of the animal kingdom. However, corresponding aberrations of nascent intelligence are seen in other vertebrates; if the abuses are less flagrant, it may be because the animals lack organs that lend themselves to destructive activities so well as does the primate hand. The most intelligent horse I ever had, whose ability to open gate fastenings of all sorts was no less amazing than it was annoying, would sometimes amuse himself by pulling shrubbery to pieces, apparently out of curiosity, as he dropped rather than ate the fragments. Less clever horses in the same pasture were never seen to do this.

The bower-birds of Australia and New Guinea differ from all other birds in building for their courtship rites elaborate structures adorned with flowers, fruits, shells, and other colorful ornaments. Even if allowance be made for the encomiums that admirers have bestowed on their intelligence and aesthetic sense, these are undoubtedly of an order exceptional among birds. It is recorded of the Satin Bower-bird of eastern Australia that males in full blue plumage deliberately tear apart the bowers of their neighbors during temporary absences of the latter, scattering the sticks and carrying off the bright ornaments to their own bowers (Marshall 1954). Although many birds, both colonial and solitary, steal pieces

Satin Bower-bird, *Ptilonorhynchus violaceus*, at his bower
with ornaments displayed on platform in front

from unguarded nests of other pairs of the same or different species, the motive in these cases is not the destruction of the neighbor's nest but the acquisition of materials for building their own. The exceptionally gifted bower-birds of this and other species are, as far as I know, the only birds that wantonly destroy the property of others of their kind, in an act that brings no immediate advantage to themselves but may disadvantage competitors for visiting females.

Captive Satin Bower-birds, deprived of the blue objects they so avidly collect for the adornment of their bowers, have sometimes killed smaller occupants of the aviary with blue in their plumage, then carried the corpses to their display stage. This, too, is very humanlike behavior; the satisfaction of an aesthetic urge, perhaps of no high order, has too often driven humans to acts of violence and destruction, of which with growing insight they become ashamed. One example of this is the vast and nefarious trade in plumage for women's hats that flourished until early in the twentieth century. In whatever kind of animal it arises, intelligence appears to pass through a stage in which it can be temporarily captured by some single motive or appetite, in the service of which it acts as though oblivious to all wider considerations. Often, at the bidding of one narrow motive, it will do things contrary to some other motive that it will soon obey.

Contemplating the many disorders to which nascent intelligence is subject and the vast amount of harm it has done, we are sometimes inclined to agree with Cicero (1951) that "it would have been better if the immortal gods had not bestowed upon us any reasoning faculty at all than that they should have bestowed it with such mischievous results." Only when its turbulent childhood passes into a strong and competent maturity will intelligence outgrow its atomism and become integrated in the service of harmonization, the central determinant of the beings in which it arises.

INTELLECTUAL MATURITY AND VITAL INTEGRITY

One confronted with the problem of liberating people from the domination of violent and disruptive passions and making them whole might suppose that this could be accomplished by giving them rules of conduct enforced by some external authority. This has been tried since early times, when the tribal mores were believed to have been established by a god who would punish the least infringement of the ordinances. But the constant angry jeremiads of the Hebrew prophets make it clear that even rules supposedly given by the one omnipotent maker and ruler of the world failed to restrain the wayward impulses of a headstrong people. Neither promises of eternal bliss nor threats of endless torments have sufficed to make humans good. All the vigilance of the law, all the force of public opinion, all the penalties that society can devise, fail to restrain men and women from excesses and to restore to them that vital integrity which must have belonged to their prehuman ancestors, as it does to other animals. Every possible use of external force or persuasion to make human conduct consistently conform to a sound and comprehensive pattern of human life has failed. The reason is clear: every living thing bears its integrating principle within itself; nothing external is an adequate substitute.

But to create a "unitary man" by impressing a stereotyped pattern of behavior upon the nervous system, somewhat in the manner of instinct-guided animals, is not a promising solution to the problem. To accomplish this, it would be necessary to reverse the course of evolution, which is an essentially irreversible process. Moreover, such a solution would deprive us of the freedom and flexibility of thought and action that humankind has struggled so long and painfully to win. We can recover the wholeness that is the birthright of many other creatures neither by external threats and inducements nor by impressing a pattern of behavior upon our nervous system, in the manner of the squirrel and the sparrow. The only promising course is to integrate our lives in accordance with an ideal of conduct inspired by harmonization and deliberately cultivated by the mind. To become good and whole, we must first create an ideal of goodness and wholeness, and cleave to it with such intense love that no other emotion can overpower it.

But we cannot win wholeness and freedom by adopting some ideal that ignores the conditions of our present existence, one of the most obvious of which is the spirit's close association with an organic body. An aspiration ignoring this insistent fact is likely to dissipate itself in vain strivings. The ideal of conduct that liberates us must be formed with full cognizance of our dual nature as an organism living in precarious balance with a mutable environment and at the same time a spiritual being whose life and aspirations can never be contained in, or limited by, the needs and appetites of the body to which it is joined. For its own continued existence and tranquility, the mind must recognize the body's needs and reconcile them with its own equally urgent needs in a way that does justice to both and ensures the success of the partnership. Thus, the ideal relationship of spirit and organism is not one of coincidence, or identity of interests, but rather one of balance—such a balance as will bring health to the body, freedom and tranquility to the mind. In the measure that it can achieve this equilibrium, the mind will fulfill its ancient obligation to guide and serve the body, yet enjoy the freedom and detachment that is its aspiration and its destiny.

Of all the lessons that the sages of ancient Hellas and India taught, none is of more perennial worth than their doctrine that we can escape the bondage to the passions in which the dawn of history found us only by the deliberate cultivation of an ideal of conduct. Doubtless they often oversimplified the problem, viewing too narrowly the whole range of interests that should be included in this ideal, failing to do justice to aspects of our nature that, when intelligently cultivated, enrich and ennoble character. These were errors of the sanguine youth of philosophy, of minds newly escaped by their own efforts from thralldom to the senses and rising so strongly on unwearied wings that they seemed capable of soaring to the stars. If they failed because the atmosphere at last became too thin to support them, they at least rose higher than most of us of a later age can follow.

We are even in danger of forgetting their lesson that only the self-directed mind, loyal to an ideal it has created or at least freely accepted, is stable, dependable, and free. Neither rules of conduct attributed to some supernatural source nor the stringent regulations of society can ever replace this capacity for complete self-guidance, which belongs to every animal equipped with its full complement of instincts, and is regained by the human mind when at long last it has passed through its troubled adolescence and comes of age.

The mature mind has liberated itself from the imperious rule of those secondary determinants of activity that we call appetites and passions, has made contact with its primary determinant, its enharmonization, and is perpetually sensitive to this influence. Such a mind has constantly before it the ideal of an inclusive harmony, which is a truer, safer, and more authoritative guide than are rules imposed from without. As parents feel that they have not fulfilled their duty to offspring until they have prepared them to live without parental guidance, so it should be the aspiration of society to produce men and women who require neither external pressure nor coercion to conduct themselves as befits a free, moral intelligence. Only by such people, who need no external governance, will society ever be adequately served or governed.

THE TRAVAIL OF CREATION

Our survey of the disorders and excesses of nascent intelligence brings poignant awareness of the almost insuperable difficulties that harmonization has had to overcome. In the beginning was the problem of gathering matter in masses that would permit some of it to participate in those higher formations of which all matter seems to be potentially capable. To start this synthesis, matter had to be condensed into bodies neither too great nor too small, at temperatures neither too high nor too low. For this a planetary system was needed; and of the difficulties involved in the construction of such a system, the small proportion of the resulting planets that in any epoch are likely to offer favorable conditions, I told in *Life Ascending* (1985).

When, finally, life arose on some of these planets, it ran into trouble by its very exuberance, which gave birth to organisms in such prodigious numbers that they clashed together and destroyed one another. An avenue of escape from this deplorable situation lay in endowing them with foreseeing minds, which, by taking a comprehensive view of the total situation, might so control the numbers and activities of living things that each could fulfill its own nature without impeding the similar striving of those around it. But to develop an adequate intelligence turned out to be one of the most difficult and hazardous of all the creative tasks; so that even today it is doubtful whether human misuse of mind will not finally ruin the living world, which intelligence might so greatly benefit.

To develop high intelligence or rationality is not enough; unless well integrated with other aspects of minds, it may be more harmful than beneficial. What we need above all is spirituality, which might be defined as the interpenetration of emotion, reason, and volition. In the spiritual person, feeling is profoundly modified by knowledge, intelligence is stimulated by the affections, and the will is guided by the perfect blending of the two. In him or her, the quality, or at least the desirability, of sensations is strongly influenced by their perceived relations, so that the most pleasant sensation becomes abhorrent rather than delightful to one who knows that it is bought at the price of suffering by other creatures, in the past or in the future. Understanding fortifies the spiritual person's determination to achieve a more harmonious life, while love intensifies the desire to understand.

The disproportionate development of one of these three aspects of mind has disastrous consequences. Intelligence divorced from love or swayed by hatred is more dangerous than blind force; an unbridled will is the cause of endless evil. What we most lack is spirituality. The increase of intelligence or intensification of feeling will benefit us only if they interpenetrate more thoroughly than at present.

Sometimes, contemplating the strife, the waste, and the pain involved in the creative process, we are filled with dismay. But what should impress us even more is the urgency and intensity of the striving for beauty, joy, and understanding that this aeonian process reveals—an urgency that will surmount the greatest obstacles to reach its goal. That this is the secret spring of the whole vast movement we can hardly doubt, because, as we mature spiritually, we who are parts of this movement feel it acting within us with irresistible force. This inner revelation of the creative energy shows it to be more closely allied to love than to intelligence. We cannot conceive how intelligence, which acts only in obedience to motives that it did not originate, could give rise to love. But love, which draws things together in harmonious union, might finally produce intelligence as an instrument to further this end. And whenever it is loyal to its source, intelligence pledges itself to serve love by promoting harmony. In the measure that it does this, it justifies the long agony of its troubled childhood.

Epilogue: The Failure of Success?

Whether in the mind's eye we survey the solar system, its nine planets floating majestically around the Sun, satellites orbiting around most of them, every celestial body remaining in its own space in a system so balanced and orderly that it has endured for ages; or through a lens we admire the filigree tracery of a snow crystal; or we reflect how our brains spontaneously integrate in meaningful figures the myriad discrete vibrations that excite the retinas of our eyes—when we contemplate all this, and many similar facts, we become convinced that, from its physical foundations to its highest developments in the realm of mind and spirit, the universe is pervaded by a movement that arranges its constituents in patterns of increasing amplitude, complexity, and coherence: the cosmic process of harmonization. While bringing order out of chaos, harmonization enriches the cosmos with values, raising bare, meaningless existence to full, significant existence. Most notably, it has covered Earth with graceful forms and bright colors and has equipped certain animals to see and enjoy all this beauty. We owe to this tireless process, the true constructive factor in the evolution of life, all that makes living precious to us. It is the source of our moral nature, the foundation of our felicity.

The growth of an organism of whatever kind is an excellent example of harmonization. By adding molecule to molecule, cell to cell, organ to organ, a plant or animal grows into an organism of great complexity. Its survival from day to day depends upon the integration of all its parts and functions into a coherent system of mutually supporting organs. Even a protozoan hardly visible to the naked eye is a very complex creature, with a nucleus and plastids performing diverse functions and, on the scale of the atoms of which it is composed, an organism of great amplitude. Large animals containing trillions of atoms and billions of cells, a great diversity of organs, all united by circulatory and nervous systems, are marvels of coherent, self-regulated complexity, such as we have not yet achieved in our most intricate machines. When we reflect upon the vast variety of organisms, the multitude of species, and the incalculable billions of individuals that cover our hospitable planet, each a product of harmonization, each a harmoniously integrated system, as it must be to remain alive and active, we recognize that on Earth harmonization has been a highly successful process.

We might expect that organisms made by the same constructive process, alike in so many ways that biologists have recognized, would, whatever their outward shape, form a harmonious community of living creatures; that the relations between all members of the immense assemblage would be as harmonious as the internal organization of each of them. Why does the process that has brought order and stability to the solar system, that aligns atoms and molecules in glittering crystals, that is active in the growth of every least organism, fail so dismally to bring concord into the relations of all these organisms? Why does the world process, instead of continuing steadily onward in the same direction, adding harmony to harmony at an ever higher level of integration, abruptly falter or reverse its course when it passes beyond the individual organism? Why does a cosmic movement having as its only goal or purpose, as far as we can tell, the enrichment of Being with high values produce so strange a mixture of values and disvalues, of good and evil? When we contemplate all the strife, carnage, and disease that afflict the living world, the fear, hatred, rage, pain, and frustration that distress us and, apparently, other animals, we sometimes suspect that pain and sorrow outweigh joy, that the farther life advances, the more it suffers. Success in covering Earth with myriad living forms fails to bring harmony among these forms, to make the living world what, in view of the process that pervades it, we might expect it to become.

The causes of this failure are not far to seek. The primary cause is the insulation of organisms. The integuments indispensable for the protection of all the delicately balanced physiological processes that preserve life make of each organism an almost closed system, independent of other similar systems. Their insulation is not only physiological but psychic: just as the malfunction or disease of one does not directly affect the health of another, so the joys and sufferings of one creature are not felt by another; one animal can agonize and die without causing the least discomfort to another of the same or a different kind. Even humans with a developed language and other means of communication often feel remote from those closest to them. Difficulty of communication often seems to separate us by interplanetary distances not only from animals of other species, including the domestic mammals and birds most intimately associated with us, but frequently from other humans— all without the admirable arrangement that keeps every planet in its course, never clashing with another.

Thus, physiological and psychic insulation makes it possible for one creature to exploit, maim, torture, or kill another without physical or mental consequences distressful to itself. Add to this the excessive abundance of organisms, which throws them into relentless competition for almost everything they need to sustain life and to reproduce, and we have the stage set for all the miseries that creatures inflict upon one another day after day and everywhere, which in aggregate far exceed all that the living world suffers from the intermittent and local excesses of lifeless nature, such as earthquakes, volcanic eruptions, hurricanes, and floods. Life's great misfortune is that evolution, dependent upon random genetic mutations that are more often harmful than beneficial, is a process in which quality too frequently wages a losing battle against quantity. Although the growth of an organism is a mode of harmonization, the organism's form and function are determined by its genetic endowment. Harmonization arranges the genes in the most coherent pattern they are capable of assuming, but it can operate only with the materials available to it.

The failure of harmonization's success in covering Earth with abundant life is not absolute, as everyone who has experienced happiness and true values should bear witness. In the foregoing chapters we noticed some of the ways in which animals cooperate to increase the safety or enhance the quality of their lives. Noteworthy are the foraging flocks of mixed species of birds, the relations between cleaner fish and their clients, the adoption of lost or orphaned young by birds and mammals, and the concord that prevails in groups of cooperatively breeding birds. Especially significant are the mutually beneficial interactions of plants and the animals that pollinate their flowers or disperse their seeds in return for food in the form of nectar or fruits. Harmonious associations can arise among individuals of the same species, of different genera or orders, of different zoological classes of animals, and even between animals and plants.

In our more optimistic moods, we may take peaceful associations as indicative of the direction in which the living world is moving, to make them more common in future ages, perhaps, if all goes well, to the virtual elimination of strife. Nevertheless, it remains true that in the present age competition and merciless exploitation are much more frequent in the animal kingdom than is harmonious cooperation. Conflict and predatory violence are so widespread and conspicuous that people have long been familiar with this harsh aspect of nature; many of the cooperative associations were unknown until, in recent times, the patient observations of naturalists disclosed them—which makes it appear probable that many more remain to be discovered.

In many ways, the most successful product of evolution and harmonization is humankind. In an exceptionally well-endowed and enduring body, well equipped with sensory organs, the human being has a large brain and an active mind. These advantages, coupled with hands that are the most versatile executive organs in the animal kingdom, enable us to fill our needs and modify our environment to our own advantage as no other animal can; to spread over every habitable region of Earth and to become by far the most abundant large terrestrial animal. Despite all these advantages, it appears that we are rushing headlong to the failure of our success, which will not be far distant if we do not promptly reverse our course. By our soaring billions, we are overexploiting the planet's productivity, devastating the environment, polluting air and soil and water. And as humans become too abundant, their average quality decreases, as is evident from the mounting crime rate, the increasing addiction to stupefying drugs, and the greater fecundity of the least competent and responsible moiety of the population.

The addition of humans to the long list of extinct animals would be lamentable because people bring to the living world qualities otherwise rare or lacking: ability to appreciate its beauty; to seek knowledge and understanding; to care devotedly and unselfishly for Earth and everything good and lovable that it contains; to feel compassion for fellow creatures of all kinds; and to be grateful for manifold blessings—all of which are attributes very unequally developed among humans.

What is needed to save humankind from self-destruction is common knowledge: population must be stabilized or, preferably, reduced by restricting the birthrate; the environment must be protected. The burning question is whether an organism physiologically and psychically insulated from all others can transcend its limiting integument to feel itself part of an encompassing whole on which its own prosperity depends; to recognize its responsibility to this whole; to feel instinctive or imaginative sympathy for other creatures; to restrain its appetites and dominate its passions in order to live more harmoniously with others. We know that some individuals are capable of cultivating this wider vision and living in its light. If a larger proportion of humanity could attain this spiritual level and the generosity that corresponds to it, success might follow success, directly for humankind, indirectly for a large segment of the living world.

An augury for success is found in the history of human intellectual development. Over the ages, we have learned not only to use our facile hands for ever more complex creative tasks but also to employ our restless minds for deeper understanding of nature. The superstitions that filled, and too often oppressed, the minds of our ancestors have, with the growth of philosophy and science, been largely dispelled from the thoughts of the more enlightened of our contemporaries, although unfortunately they linger stubbornly in a large part of humanity. Our success in clarifying our thoughts and combatting many of the diseases that afflicted our progenitors should encourage us to tackle more resolutely the immense and yearly growing problems that confront humanity but are not intrinsically insoluble. What is lacking is the foresight and the will to make Earth a fit abode for the children that we beget in excessive numbers, for their remote descendants, and for the many creatures that might dwell compatibly with them.

Bibliography

Allee, W. C. 1951. *Cooperation among animals*. New York: Henry Schuman.

Belt, T. 1888. *The naturalist in Nicaragua*, 2nd. ed. London: Edward Bumpus.

Bourlière, F. 1954. *The natural history of mammals*. New York: Alfred A. Knopf.

Breasted, J. H. 1933. *The dawn of conscience*. New York: Charles Scribner's Sons.

Brocher, F. 1911. Le problème de l'utriculaire. *Ann. de Biol. Lacustre* 5:36–46.

Brown, J. L. 1987. *Helping and communal breeding in birds*. Princeton, N.J.: Princeton University Press.

Bühler, K. 1930. *The mental development of the child*. London: Routledge and Kegan Paul.

Burkhardt, F., D. M. Porter, J. Browne, and M. Richmond, eds. 1993. *The correspondence of Charles Darwin*, vol. 8. 1960. Cambridge, U.K.: Cambridge University Press.

Büsgen, M. 1888. Ueber die Art und Bedeutung des Tierfangs bei *Utricularia vulgaris L. Ber. der deutsch bot. Gesellschaft* 6:lv–lxiii.

Carpenter, C. R. 1934. A field study of the behavior and social relations of howling monkeys (*Alouatta palliata*). *Comparative Psychology Monogr.* 10:1–168.

Childe, G. 1942. *What happened in history*. Harmondsworth, Middlesex: Penguin Books.

Cicero, M. T. 1951. *De natura deorum*. Trans. by H. Rackham. Cambridge, Mass.: Harvard University Press.

Conder, P. S. 1949. Individual distance. *Ibis* 91:649–55.

Conway, W. G. 1965. Apartment-building and cliff-dwelling parrots. *Animal Kingdom* 68:40–46.

Crouan Frères. 1858. Observations sur un mode particulier de propagation des *Utricularia*. *Bull. Soc. Bot. de France* 5:27–29.

Czaja, A. F. 1922. Die Fangvorrichtung der Utriculariablase. *Zeit. für Bot.* 14:705–29.

Darwin, C. 1875. *Insectivorous Plants*. Reprint 1897, New York: D. Appleton and Co.

Dawkins, R. 1976. *The selfish gene*. New York and Oxford: Oxford University Press.

Dobie, J. F. 1945. *Strange animal friendships*. Nature Mag. 38:9–12.

Dorst, J. 1962. Nouvelles recherches biologiques sur les Trochilidés des hautes Andes péruviennes. *L'Oiseau et R.F.O.* 32:95–126.

Ekambaram, T. 1916. Irritability of the bladders in *Utricularia*. *Agric. Journ. India* 11:72–79.

Fabre, J. M. 1924. *Insect adventures: Retold for young people by L. S. Hasbrouck*. New York: Dodd, Mead.

Fisher, R. A. 1958. *The genetical theory of natural selection*. 2nd. ed. New York: Dover Publications.

Frazer, J. G. 1922. *The golden bough: A study in magic and religion*. New York: Macmillan.

Friedmann, H. 1930. The Sociable Weaver bird of South Africa. *Natural History* 30:205–12.

Hebb, D. O. 1953. Heredity and environment in mammalian behaviour. *British Journ. Animal Behaviour* 1:43–47.

Hegner, R. W. 1926. The interrelations of protozoa and the utricules of *Utricularia*. *Biol. Bull.* (Woods Hole) 50:239–70.

Howell, T. R. 1979. Breeding biology of the Egyptian Plover. *Univ. California Publ. Zool.* 113:1–76.

Immelmann, K. 1966. Beobachtungen an Schwalbenstaren. *Journ. für Ornith.* 107:37–69.

Johnson, R. A. 1969. Hatching behavior of the Bobwhite. *Wilson Bull.* 81:79–86.

Jolly, A. 1967. Malagasy lemurs: Clues to our past. *Animal Kingdom* 70:66–75.

Kipling, J. L. 1892. *Beast and man in India: A popular sketch of Indian animals and their relations with the people.* London: Macmillan.

Knorr, O. A. 1957. Communal roosting of the Pygmy Nuthatch. *Condor* 59:398.

Köhler, W. 1927. *The mentality of apes.* London: Routledge and Kegan Paul.

Kropotkin, P. 1902. *Mutual aid: A factor in evolution.* London: William Heinemann.

Lawrence, L. de K. 1968. *The lovely and the wild.* New York: McGraw-Hill.

Lloyd, F. E. 1942. *The carnivorous plants.* Waltham, Mass.: Chronica Botanica Co.

Lorenz, K. Z. 1952. *King Solomon's ring: New light on animal ways.* London: Methuen.

Maeterlinck, M. 1927. *The life of the white ant.* Trans. Alfred Sutre. New York: Dodd, Mead.

Marshall, A. J. 1954. *Bower-birds: Their displays and breeding cycles.* Oxford: Clarendon Press.

Mayr, E. 1988. *Toward a new philosophy of biology: Observations of an evolutionist.* Cambridge, Mass.: Belknap Press of Harvard University Press.

Mencius. 1942. *The book of Mencius.* Trans. by Lionel Giles. London: John Murray.

Merl, E. M. 1922. Biologische Studien über die Utriculariablase. *Flora* 15 (NF):59–74.

Meyerriecks, A. J. 1957. "Bunching" reaction of Cedar Waxwings to attacks by a Cooper's Hawk. *Wilson Bull.* 69:184.

Regan, T. 1983. *The case for animal rights.* Berkeley: University of California Press.

Riney, T. 1951. Relationships between birds and deer. *Condor* 53:178–85.

Rowley, I. 1965. *Life history of the Superb Blue Wren.* Emu 64:251–97.

Russell, B. 1917. *Mysticism and logic and other essays*. London: George Allen and Unwin.

Schjelderup-Ebbe, T. 1922. Beiträge zur Sozialpsychologie des Haushuhns. *Zeitschr. für Psychol.* 88:225–52.

Shoemaker, H. H. 1939. Social hierarchy in flocks of the Canary. *Auk* 56:381–406.

Skutch, A. F. 1928. The capture of prey by the bladderwort. *New Phytologist* 27:261–97.

———. 1983. *Birds of tropical America*. Austin: University of Texas Press.

———. 1985. *Life ascending*. Austin: University of Texas Press.

———. 1987. *Helpers at birds' nests: A worldwide survey of cooperative breeding and related behavior*. Iowa City: University of Iowa Press.

———. 1989. *Birds asleep*. Austin: University of Texas Press.

———. 1992. *Origins of nature's beauty*. Austin: University of Texas Press.

Snow, B., and D. Snow. 1988. *Birds and berries*. Calton, Staffordshire: T. and A. D. Poyser.

Stacey, P. B., and W. D. Koenig, eds. 1990. *Cooperative breeding in birds*. Cambridge: Cambridge University Press.

Tinbergen, N. 1951. *The study of instinct*. Oxford: Clarendon Press.

———. 1958. *Curious naturalists*. London: Country Life.

Van Lawick-Goodall, J. 1971. *In the shadow of man*. Boston: Houghton Mifflin.

Van Someren, V. G. L. 1956. *Days with birds: Studies of habits of some East African species*. Fieldiana, Zoology 38. Chicago: Chicago Natural History Museum.

Verbeek, N. A. M., and R. W. Butler. 1981. Cooperative breeding of the Northwestern Crow, *Corvus caurinus*, in British Columbia. Ibis 123:183–89.

Wallace, A. R. 1872. *The Malay Archipelago*. London: Macmillan.

Weigum, L. 1970. Seladang. *Animal Kingdom* 73:2–9.

Wheeler, W. M. 1928. *The social insects: Their origin and evolution*. New York: Harcourt, Brace.

Wickler, W. 1968. *El mimetismo en las plantas y en los animales* (Translation of *Mimikry: Signalfälschungen der Natur*). Mexico City: McGraw-Hill.

Wilkinson, R. 1982. Social organization and communal breeding in the Chestnut-bellied Starling (*Spreo pulcher*). *Animal Behav.* 30:1118–28.

Willis, E. O. 1967. The behavior of Bicolored Antbirds. *Univ. California Publ. Zool.* 79:1–132.

Withycombe, C. L. 1926. Observations on the bladderwort. *Knowledge* 15:238–41.

Woodruff, L. L. 1922. *Foundations of biology.* New York: Macmillan.

Woolfenden, G. E. 1975. Florida Scrub Jay helpers at the nest. *Auk* 92:1–15.

Wright, S. 1940. "The statistical consequences of Mendelian heredity in relation to speciation." In *The new systematics*, ed. J. Huxley. Oxford: Oxford University Press.

———. 1949. "Adaptation and selection." In *Genetics, paleontology, and evolution*, ed. G. L. Jepsen, E. Mayr, and G. G. Simpson. Princeton, N.J.: Princeton University Press.

Index

Humans, humankind: auguries of salvation of, 201–202; excessive abundance of, 201; relations with plants, 87–88; threatened disaster of, 201; tribal life of, 95
Hummingbirds, 28, 158
Hunger: as cause of conflict, 37–39
Huntsman's Cup, *Sarracenia purpurea*, 99, **100**
Hydra, Green, 129
Hymenoptera, 64; social bonds of, 70

Ideals: barbarous, 182–87; need of, 190–93
Ikhnaton, 178
Immelmann, Klaus, 64
Individual distance of birds: as mobile territory, 64
Insects: abundance of, 85; exploitation of plants by, 85; number of species of, 85
Instinct: and learning, 165; phases of, 166–68; and reflex action, 164–65; subordination to intelligence of, 169–71
Insulation of organisms: consequences of, 3–8, 199
Intellectual maturity: and vital integrity, 190–92
Intelligence, 169–71; aberrations of dawning, 187–90; of animals, 187–90; disillusion of, 186–87; gigantic task of nascent, 171–72; rank growth of special motives of, 179–82; tragic mistake of nascent, 172–75
Intergroup selection, 131, 143–50; absence of in vegerative multiplication, 147; changing attitudes toward, 150; compared with interindividual selection, 143–45; and cooperative breeding, 146–47; measures of fitness in, 143–44; and sexual reproduction,

46–47; transcends specific limits, 149
Isaiah, 39

Jacaranda trees, *Jacaranda* spp., 81
Jackals, *Canis aureus*, 77
Jackdaw, *Corvus monedula*, 61
Jackfish, Crevalle, 58
Jay, Brown, *Cyanocorax morio:* cooperative breeding of, 75
European, *Garrulus glandarius:* social relations of, 61
Florida scrub, *Aphelocoma coerulescens:* cooperative breeding of, 75
Johnson, Robert A., 76
Jolly, Alison, 66

Kipling, John Lockwood, 38
Knorr, Owen A., 71
Köhler, Wolfgang, 171, 187–88
Kropotkin, Petr Aleksyeevich, 54, 77

Labroides dimidiatus, 68
Language: effects of, 95–96; origins of, 95
Langurs, *Presbytis* spp., brutality of, 25
Lawrence, Louise de Kiriline, 69
Leks, 28. *See also* courtship assemblies
Lemurs: grooming by, 66
Lentibulariaceae, 108
Lianas: aggressiveness of, 81, 84
Life, or living organisms: adaptation to environment of, 12; conflicts of, 13–14; consequences of insulation of, 1–8; toughness and aggressiveness of, 8–13
Lions, *Felis leo:* brutality of, 25
Lizard, Iguana, 86
Lloyd, Francis E., 126
Loranthaceae, 82
Lorenz, Konrad Z., 38, 61
Love: as expression of creative energy, 194–95